Marx Hardy Abbott Defoe Melville Machiavelli Montaigne Chesterton Cooper Emerson Joyce Austen Hugo Eliot Grimm Haggard Carroll Christie Stoker Wilde Maupassant Byron Molière Schiller Engels Garnett Goethe Einstein Fitzgerald Hawthorne Smith Kafka Hall Dostoyevsky Willis Cotton Kipling Doyle Baum Henry Nietzsche Leslie Dumas Flaubert Turgenev Balzac Stockton Vatsyayana Crane Burroughs Verne Curtis Tocqueville Whitman Gogol Vinci Homer Widger Tolstoy Busch Darwin Thoreau Twain Potter Freud Zola Lawrence Scott Plato Harte Kant Jowett Stevenson Dickens Andersen London Descartes Cervantes Burton Hesse Poe Aristotle Wells Voltaire Hale James Hastings Cooke Bunner Shakespeare Irving Richter Chambers da Doré Dante Chekhov Shaw Wodehouse Benedict Alcott Pushkin Newton Swift

 **tredition**

tredition was established in 2006 by Sandra Latusseck and Soenke Schulz. Based in Hamburg, Germany, tredition offers publishing solutions to authors and publishing houses, combined with worldwide distribution of printed and digital book content. tredition is uniquely positioned to enable authors and publishing houses to create books on their own terms and without conventional manufacturing risks.

For more information please visit: www.tredition.com

TREDITION CLASSICS

This book is part of the TREDITION CLASSICS series. The creators of this series are united by passion for literature and driven by the intention of making all public domain books available in printed format again - worldwide. Most TREDITION CLASSICS titles have been out of print and off the bookstore shelves for decades. At tredition we believe that a great book never goes out of style and that its value is eternal. Several mostly non-profit literature projects provide content to tredition. To support their good work, tredition donates a portion of the proceeds from each sold copy. As a reader of a TREDITION CLASSICS book, you support our mission to save many of the amazing works of world literature from oblivion. See all available books at www.tredition.com.

Project Gutenberg

The content for this book has been graciously provided by Project Gutenberg. Project Gutenberg is a non-profit organization founded by Michael Hart in 1971 at the University of Illinois. The mission of Project Gutenberg is simple: To encourage the creation and distribution of eBooks. Project Gutenberg is the first and largest collection of public domain eBooks.

Memoirs of Marguerite de Valois —Volume 2 [Court memoir series]

Queen, consort of Henry IV, King of France Marguerite

Imprint

This book is part of TREDITION CLASSICS

Author: Queen, consort of Henry IV, King of France Marguerite
Cover design: Buchgut, Berlin – Germany

Publisher: tredition GmbH, Hamburg - Germany
ISBN: 978-3-8424-5329-6

www.tredition.com
www.tredition.de

MARGUERITE DE NAVARRE

MEMOIRS OF MARGUERITE DE VALOIS

MEMOIRS OF MARGUERITE DE VALOIS QUEEN OF NAVARRE

Written by Herself

Being Historic Memoirs of the Courts of France and Navarre

BOOK II.

LETTER XIII.

The League.—War Declared against the Huguenots.—Queen Marguerite Sets out for Spa.

At length my brother returned to Court, accompanied by all the Catholic nobility who had followed his fortunes. The King received him very graciously, and showed, by his reception of him, how much he was pleased at his return. Bussi, who returned with my brother, met likewise with a gracious reception. Le Guast was now no more, having died under the operation of a particular regimen ordered for him by his physician. He had given himself up to every kind of debauchery; and his death seemed the judgment of the Almighty on one whose body had long been perishing, and whose soul had been made over to the prince of demons as the price of assistance through the means of diabolical magic, which he constantly practised. The King, though now without this instrument of his malicious contrivances, turned his thoughts entirely upon the destruction of the Huguenots. To effect this, he strove to engage my brother against them, and thereby make them his enemies and that I might be considered as another enemy, he used every means to prevent me from going to the King my husband. Accordingly he showed every mark of attention to both of us, and manifested an inclination to gratify all our wishes.

After some time, M. de Duras arrived at Court, sent by the King my husband to hasten my departure. Hereupon, I pressed the King greatly to think well of it, and give me his leave. He, to colour his refusal, told me he could not part with me at present, as I was the chief ornament of his Court; that he must, keep me a little longer, after which he would accompany me himself on my way as far as Poitiers. With this answer and assurance, he sent M. de Duras back.

These excuses were purposely framed in order to gain time until everything was prepared for declaring war against the Huguenots, and, in consequence, against the King my husband, as he fully designed to do.

As a pretence to break with the Huguenots, a report was spread abroad that the Catholics were dissatisfied with the Peace of Sens, and thought the terms of it too advantageous for the Huguenots. This rumour succeeded, and produced all that discontent amongst the Catholics intended by it. A league was formed: in the provinces and great cities, which was joined by numbers of the Catholics. M. de Guise was named as the head of all. This was well known to the King, who pretended to be ignorant of what was going forward, though nothing else was talked of at Court.

The States were convened to meet at Blois. Previous to the opening of this assembly, the King called my brother to his closet, where were present the Queen my mother and some of the King's counsellors. He represented the great consequence the Catholic league was to his State and authority, even though they should appoint De Guise as the head of it; that such a measure was of the highest importance to them both, meaning my brother and himself; that the Catholics had very just reason to be dissatisfied with the peace, and that it behoved him, addressing himself to my brother, rather to join the Catholics than the Huguenots, and this from conscience as well as interest. He concluded his address to my brother with conjuring him, as a son of France and a good Catholic, to assist him with his aid and counsel in this critical juncture, when his crown and the Catholic religion were both at stake. He further said that, in order to get the start of so formidable a league, he ought to form one himself, and become the head of it, as well to show his zeal for religion as to prevent the Catholics from uniting under any other leader. He then proposed to declare himself the head of a league, which should be joined by my brother, the princes, nobles, governors, and others holding offices under the Government. Thus was my brother reduced to the necessity of making his Majesty a tender of his services for the support and maintenance of the Catholic religion.

The King, having now obtained assurances of my brother's assistance in the event of a war, which was his sole view in the league which he had formed with so much art, assembled together the princes and chief noblemen of his Court, and, calling for the roll of the league, signed it first himself, next calling upon my brother to sign it, and, lastly, upon all present.

The next day the States opened their meeting, when the King, calling upon the Bishops of Lyons, Ambrune, Vienne, and other prelates there present, for their advice, was told that, after the oath taken at his coronation, no oath made to heretics could bind him, and therefore he was absolved from his engagements with the Huguenots.

This declaration being made at the opening of the assembly, and war declared against the Huguenots, the King abruptly dismissed from Court the Huguenot, Genisac, who had arrived a few days before, charged by the King my husband with a commission to hasten my departure. The King very sharply told him that his sister had been given to a Catholic, and not to a Huguenot; and that if the King my husband expected to have me, he must declare himself a Catholic.

Every preparation for war was made, and nothing else talked of at Court; and, to make my brother still more obnoxious to the Huguenots, he had the command of an army given him. Genisac came and informed me of the rough message he had been dismissed with. Hereupon I went directly to the closet of the Queen my mother, where I found the King. I expressed my resentment at being deceived by him, and at being cajoled by his promise to accompany me from Paris to Poitiers, which, as it now appeared, was a mere pretence. I represented that I did not marry by my own choice, but entirely agreeable to the advice of King Charles, the Queen my mother, and himself; that, since they had given him to me for a husband, they ought not to hinder me from partaking of his fortunes; that I was resolved to go to him, and that if I had not their leave, I would get away how I could, even at the hazard of my life. The King answered: "Sister, it is not now a time to importune me for leave. I acknowledge that I have, as you say, hitherto prevented you from going, in order to forbid it altogether. From the time the King of Navarre changed his religion, and again became a Huguenot, I have been against your going to him. What the Queen my mother and I are doing is for your good. I am determined to carry on a war of extermination until this wretched religion of the Huguenots, which is of so mischievous a nature, is no more. Consider, my sister, if you, who are a Catholic, were once in their hands, you would become a hostage for me, and prevent my design. And who knows but they might seek their revenge upon me by taking away your life? No, you shall not go amongst them; and if you leave us in the manner you have now mentioned, rely upon it that you will make the Queen your mother and me your bitterest enemies, and that we shall use every means to make you feel the effects of our resentment; and, moreover, you will make your husband's situation worse instead of better."

I went from this audience with much dissatisfaction, and, taking advice of the principal persons of both sexes belonging to Court whom I esteemed my friends, I found them all of opinion that it would be exceedingly improper for me to remain in a Court now at open variance with the King my husband. They recommended me not to stay at Court whilst the war lasted, saying it would be more honourable for me to leave the kingdom under the pretence of a pilgrimage, or a visit to some of my kindred. The Princesse de Roche-sur-Yon was amongst those I consulted upon the occasion, who was on the point of setting off for Spa to take the waters there.

My brother was likewise present at the consultation, and brought with him Mondoucet, who had been to Flanders in quality of the King's agent, whence he was just returned to represent to the King the discontent that had arisen amongst the Flemings on account of infringements made by the Spanish Government on the French laws. He stated that he was commissioned by several nobles, and the municipalities of several towns, to declare how much they were inclined in their hearts towards France, and how ready they were to come under a French government. Mondoucet, perceiving the King not inclined to listen to his representation, as having his mind wholly occupied by the war he had entered into with the Huguenots, whom he was resolved to punish for having joined my brother, had ceased to move in it further to the King, and addressed himself on the subject to my brother. My brother, with that princely spirit which led him to undertake great achievements, readily lent an ear to Mondoucet's proposition, and promised to engage in it, for he was born rather to conquer than to keep what he conquered. Mondoucet's proposition was the more pleasing to him as it was not unjust, it being, in fact, to recover to France what had been usurped by Spain.

Mondoucet had now engaged himself in my brother's service, and was to return to Flanders' under a pretence of accompanying the Princesse de Roche-sur-Yon in her journey to Spa; and as this agent perceived my counsellers to be at a loss for some pretence for my leaving Court and quitting France during the war, and that at first Savoy was proposed for my retreat, then Lorraine, and then Our Lady of Loretto, he suggested to my brother that I might be of great use to him in Flanders, if, under the colour of any complaint, I should be recommended to drink the Spa waters, and go with the Princesse de Roche-sur-Yon. My brother acquiesced in this opinion, and came up to me, saying: "Oh, Queen! you need be no longer at a loss for a place to go to. I have observed that you have frequently an erysipelas on your arm, and you must accompany the Princess to Spa. You must say, your physicians had ordered those waters for the complaint; but when they, did so, it was not the season to take them. That season is now approaching, and you hope to have the King's leave to go there."

My brother did not deliver all he wished to say at that time, because the
Cardinal de Bourbon was present, whom he knew to be a friend to the
Guises and to Spain. However, I saw through his real design, and that he
wished me to promote his views in Flanders.

The company approved of my brother's advice, and the Princesse de Roche-sur-Yon heard the proposal with great joy, having a great regard for me. She promised to attend me to the Queen my mother when I should ask her consent.

The next day I found the Queen alone, and represented to her the extreme regret I experienced in finding that a war was inevitable betwixt the King my husband and his Majesty, and that I must continue in a state of separation from my husband; that, as long as the war lasted, it was neither decent nor honourable for me to stay at Court, where I must be in one or other, or both, of these cruel situations either that the King my husband should believe that I continued in it out of inclination, and think me deficient in the duty I owed him; or that his Majesty should entertain suspicions of my giving intelligence to the King my husband. Either of these cases, I observed, could not but prove injurious to me. I therefore prayed her not to take it amiss if I desired to remove myself from Court, and from becoming so unpleasantly situated; adding that my physicians had for some time recommended me to take the Spa waters for an erysipelas—to which I had been long subject—on my arm; the season for taking these waters was now approaching, and that if she approved of it, I would use the present opportunity, by which means I should be at a distance from Court, and show my husband that, as I could not be with him, I was unwilling to remain amongst his enemies. I further expressed my hopes that, through her prudence, a peace might be effected in a short time betwixt the King my husband and his Majesty, and that my husband might be restored to the favour he formerly enjoyed; that whenever I learned the news of so joyful an event, I would renew my solicitations to be permitted to go to my husband. In the meantime, I should hope for her permission to have the honour of accompanying the Princesse de Roche-sur-Yon, there present, in her journey to Spa.

She approved of what I proposed, and expressed her satisfaction that I had taken so prudent a resolution. She observed how much she was chagrined when she found that the King, through the evil persuasions of the bishops, had resolved to break through the conditions of the last peace, which she had concluded in his name. She saw already the ill effects of this hasty proceeding, as it had removed from the King's Council many of his ablest and best servants. This gave her, she said, much concern, as it did likewise to think I could not remain at Court without offending my husband, or creating jealousy and suspicion in the King's mind. This being certainly what was likely to be the consequence of my staying, she would advise the King to give me leave to set out on this journey.

She was as good as her word, and the King discoursed with me on the subject without exhibiting the smallest resentment. Indeed, he was well pleased now that he had prevented me from going to the King my husband, for whom he had conceived the greatest animosity.

He ordered a courier to be immediately despatched to Don John of Austria, — who commanded for the King of Spain in Flanders, — to obtain from him the necessary passports for a free passage in the countries under his command, as I should be obliged to cross a part of Flanders to reach Spa, which is in the bishopric of Liege.

All matters being thus arranged, we separated in a few days after this interview. The short time my brother and I remained together was employed by him in giving me instructions for the commission I had undertaken to execute for him in Flanders. The King and the Queen my mother set out for Poitiers, to be near the army of M. de Mayenne, then besieging Brouage, which place being reduced, it was intended to march into Gascony and attack the King my husband.

My brother had the command of another army, ordered to besiege Issoire and some other towns, which he soon after took.

For my part, I set out on my journey to Flanders accompanied by the Princesse de Roche-sur-Yon, Madame de Tournon, the lady of my bedchamber, Madame de Mouy of Picardy, Madame de Chastelaine, De Millon, Mademoiselle d'Atric, Mademoiselle de Tournon, and seven or eight other young ladies. My male attendants were the Cardinal de Lenoncourt, the Bishop of Langres, and M. de Mouy, Seigneur de Picardy, at present father-in-law to the brother of Queen Louise, called the Comte de Chalingy, with my principal steward of the household, my chief esquires, and the other gentlemen of my establishment.

LETTER XIV.

Description of Queen Marguerite's Equipage.—Her Journey to Liege Described.—She Enters with Success upon Her Mission.—Striking Instance of Maternal Duty and Affection in a Great Lady.—Disasters near the Close of the Journey.

The cavalcade that attended me excited great curiosity as it passed through the several towns in the course of my journey, and reflected no small degree of credit on France, as it was splendidly set out, and made a handsome appearance. I travelled in a litter raised with pillars. The lining of it was Spanish velvet, of a crimson colour, embroidered in various devices with gold and different coloured silk thread.

The windows were of glass, painted in devices. The lining and windows had, in the whole, forty devices, all different and alluding to the sun and its effects. Each device had its motto, either in the Spanish or Italian language. My litter was followed by two others; in the one was the Princesse de Roche-sur-Yon, and in the other Madame de Tournon, my lady of the bedchamber. After them followed ten maids of honour, on horseback, with their governess; and, last of all, six coaches and chariots, with the rest of the ladies and all our female attendants.

I took the road of Picardy, the towns in which province had received the King's orders to pay me all due honours. Being arrived at Le Catelet, a strong place, about three leagues distant from the frontier of the Cambresis, the Bishop of Cambray (an ecclesiastical State acknowledging the King of Spain only as a guarantee) sent a gentleman to inquire of me at what hour I should leave the place, as he intended to meet me on the borders of his territory.

Accordingly I found him there, attended by a number of his people, who appeared to be true Flemings, and to have all the rusticity and unpolished manners of their country. The Bishop was of the

House of Barlemont, one of the principal families in Flanders. All of this house have shown themselves Spaniards at heart, and at that time were firmly attached to Don John. The Bishop received me with great politeness and not a little of the Spanish ceremony.

Although the city of Cambray is not so well built as some of our towns in France, I thought it, notwithstanding, far more pleasant than many of these, as the streets and squares are larger and better disposed. The churches are grand and highly ornamented, which is, indeed, common to France; but what I admired, above all, was the citadel, which is the finest and best constructed in Christendom.

The Spaniards experienced it to be strong whilst my brother had it in his possession. The governor of the citadel at this time was a worthy gentleman named M. d'Ainsi, who was, in every respect, a polite and well-accomplished man, having the carriage and behaviour of one of our most perfect courtiers, very different from the rude incivility which appears to be the characteristic of a Fleming.

The Bishop gave us a grand supper, and after supper a ball, to which he had invited all the ladies of the city. As soon as the ball was opened he withdrew, in accordance with the Spanish ceremony; but M. d'Ainsi did the honours for him, and kept me company during the ball, conducting me afterwards to a collation, which, considering his command at the citadel, was, I thought, imprudent. I speak from experience, having been taught, to my cost, and contrary to my desire, the caution and vigilance necessary to be observed in keeping such places. As my regard for my brother was always predominant in me, I continually had his instructions in mind, and now thought I had a fair opportunity to open my commission and forward his views in Flanders, this town of Cambray, and especially the citadel, being, as it were, a key to that country. Accordingly I employed all the talents God had given me to make M. d'Ainsi a friend to France, and attach him to my brother's interest. Through God's assistance I succeeded with him, and so much was M. d'Ainsi pleased with my conversation that he came to the resolution of soliciting the Bishop, his master, to grant him leave to accompany me as, far as Namur, where Don John of Austria was in waiting to receive me, observing that he had a great desire to witness so splendid an interview. This Spanish Fleming, the Bishop, had the weakness to grant M. d'Ainsi's request, who continued following in my train for ten or twelve days. During this time he took every opportunity of discoursing with me, and showed that, in his heart, he was well disposed to embrace the service of France, wishing no better master than the Prince my brother, and declaring that he heartily despised being under the command of his Bishop, who, though his sovereign, was not his superior by birth, being born a private gentleman like himself, and, in every other respect, greatly his inferior.

Leaving Cambray, I set out to sleep at Valenciennes, the chief city of a part of Flanders called by the same name. Where this country is divided from Cambresis (as far as which I was conducted by the Bishop of Cambray), the Comte de Lalain, M. de Montigny his brother, and a number of gentlemen, to the amount of two or three hundred, came to meet me.

Valenciennes is a town inferior to Cambray in point of strength, but equal to it for the beauty of its squares, and churches, — the former ornamented with fountains, as the latter are with curious clocks. The ingenuity of the Germans in the construction of their clocks was a matter of great surprise to all my attendants, few amongst whom had ever before seen clocks exhibiting a number of moving figures, and playing a variety of tunes in the most agreeable manner.

The Comte de Lalain, the governor of the city, invited the lords and gentlemen of my train to a banquet, reserving himself to give an entertainment to the ladies on our arrival at Mons, where we should find the Countess his wife, his sister-in-law Madame d'Aurec, and other ladies of distinction. Accordingly the Count, with his attendants, conducted us thither the next day. He claimed a relationship with the King my husband, and was, in reality, a person who carried great weight and authority. He was much dissatisfied with the Spanish Government, and had conceived a great dislike for it since the execution of Count Egmont, who was his near kinsman.

Although he had hitherto abstained from entering into the league with the Prince of Orange and the Huguenots, being himself a steady Catholic, yet he had not admitted of an interview with Don

John, neither would he suffer him, nor any one in the interest of Spain, to enter upon his territories. Don John was unwilling to give the Count any umbrage, lest he should force him to unite the Catholic League of Flanders, called the League of the States, to that of the Prince of Orange and the Huguenots, well foreseeing that such a union would prove fatal to the Spanish interest, as other governors have since experienced. With this disposition of mind, the Comte de Lalain thought he could not give me sufficient demonstrations of the joy he felt by my presence; and he could not have shown more honour to his natural prince, nor displayed greater marks of zeal and affection.

On our arrival at Mons, I was lodged in his house, and found there the Countess his wife, and a Court consisting of eighty or a hundred ladies of the city and country. My reception was rather that of their sovereign lady than of a foreign princess. The Flemish ladies are naturally lively, affable, and engaging. The Comtesse de Lalain is remarkably so, and is, moreover, a woman of great sense and elevation of mind, in which particular, as well as in air and countenance, she carries a striking resemblance to the lady your cousin. We became immediately intimate, and commenced a firm friendship at our first meeting. When the supper hour came, we sat down to a banquet, which was succeeded by a ball; and this rule the Count observed as long as I stayed at Mons, which was, indeed, longer than I intended. It had been my intention to stay at Mons one night only, but the Count's obliging lady prevailed on me to pass a whole week there. I strove to excuse myself from so long a stay, imagining it might be inconvenient to them; but whatever I could say availed nothing with the Count and his lady, and I was under the necessity of remaining with them eight days. The Countess and I were on so familiar a footing that she stayed in my bedchamber till a late hour, and would not have left me then had she not imposed upon herself a task very rarely performed by persons of her rank, which, however, placed the goodness of her disposition in the most amiable light. In fact, she gave suck to her infant son; and one day at table, sitting next me, whose whole attention was absorbed in the promotion of my brother's interest,—the table being the place where, according to the custom of the country, all are familiar and ceremony is laid aside,—she, dressed out in the richest manner and blazing with diamonds, gave the breast to her child without rising from her seat, the infant being brought to the table as superbly habited as its nurse, the mother. She performed this maternal duty with so much good humour, and with a gracefulness peculiar to herself, that this charitable office—which would have appeared disgusting and been considered as an affront if done by some others of equal rank—gave pleasure to all who sat at table, and, accordingly, they signified their approbation by their applause.

The tables being removed, the dances commenced in the same room wherein we had supped, which was magnificent and large. The Countess and I sitting side by side, I expressed the pleasure I received from her conversation, and that I should place this meeting amongst the happiest events of my life. "Indeed," said I, "I shall have cause to regret that it ever did take place, as I shall depart hence so unwillingly, there being so little probability, of our meeting again soon. Why did Heaven deny, our being born in the same country!"

This was said in order to introduce my brother's business. She replied: "This country did, indeed, formerly belong to France, and our lawyers now plead their causes in the French language. The greater part of the people here still retain an affection for the French nation. For my part," added the Countess, "I have had a strong attachment to your country ever since I have had the honour of seeing you. This country has been long in the possession of the House of Austria, but the regard of the people for that house has been greatly, weakened by the death of Count Egmont, M. de Horne, M. de Montigny, and others of the same party, some of them our near relations, and all of the best families of the country. We entertain the utmost dislike for the Spanish Government, and wish for nothing so much as to throw off the yoke of their tyranny; but, as the country is divided betwixt different religions, we are at a loss how to effect it if we could unite, we should soon drive out the Spaniards; but this division amongst ourselves renders us weak. Would to God the King your brother would come to a resolution of reconquering this country, to which he has an ancient claim! We should all receive him with open arms."

This was a frank declaration, made by the Countess without premeditation, but it had been long agitated in the minds of the people, who considered that it was from France they were to hope for redress from the evils with which they were afflicted. I now found I had as favourable an opening as I could wish for to declare my errand. I told her that the King of France my brother was averse to engaging in foreign war, and the more so as the Huguenots in his kingdom were too strong to admit of his sending any large force out of it. "My brother Alencon," said I, "has sufficient means, and might be induced to undertake it. He has equal valour, prudence, and benevolence with the King my brother or any of his ancestors. He has been bred to arms, and is esteemed one of the bravest generals of these times. He has the command of the King's army against the Huguenots, and has lately taken a well-fortified town, called Issoire, and some other places that were in their possession. You could not invite to your assistance a prince who has it so much in his power to give it; being not only a neighbour, but having a kingdom like France at his devotion, whence he may expect to derive the necessary aid and succour. The Count your husband may be assured that if he do my brother this good office he will not find him ungrateful, but may set what price he pleases upon his meritorious service. My brother is of a noble and generous disposition, and ready to requite those who do him favours. He is, moreover, an admirer of men of honour and gallantry, and accordingly is followed by the bravest and best men France has to boast of. I am in hopes that a peace will soon be reestablished with the Huguenots, and expect to find it so on my return to France. If the Count your husband think as you do, and will permit me to speak to him on the subject, I will engage to bring my brother over to the proposal, and, in that case, your country in general, and your house in particular, will be well satisfied with him. If, through your means, my brother should establish himself here, you may depend on seeing me often, there being no brother or sister who has a stronger affection for each other."

The Countess appeared to listen to what I said with great pleasure, and acknowledged that she had not entered upon this discourse without design. She observed that, having perceived I did her the honour to have some regard for her, she had resolved within herself not to let me depart out of the country without explaining to me the situation of it, and begging me to procure the aid of France to relieve them from the apprehensions of living in a state of perpetual war or of submitting to Spanish tyranny. She thereupon entreated me to allow her to relate our present conversation to her husband, and permit them both to confer with me on the subject the next day. To this I readily gave my consent.

Thus we passed the evening in discourse upon the object of my mission, and I observed that she took a singular pleasure in talking upon it in all our succeeding conferences when I thought proper to introduce it. The ball being ended, we went to hear vespers at the church of the Canonesses, an order of nuns of which we have none in France. These are young ladies who are entered in these communities at a tender age, in order to improve their fortunes till they are of an age to be married. They do not all sleep under the same roof, but in detached houses within an enclosure. In each of these houses are three, four, or perhaps six young girls, under the care of an old woman. These governesses, together with the abbess, are of the number of such as have never been married. These girls never wear the habit of the order but in church; and the service there ended, they dress like others, pay visits, frequent balls, and go where they please. They were constant visitors at the Count's entertainments, and danced at his balls.

The Countess thought the time long until the night, when she had an opportunity of relating to the Count the conversation she had with me, and the opening of the business. The next morning she came to me, and brought her husband with her. He entered into a detail of the grievances the country laboured under, and the just reasons he had for ridding it of the tyranny of Spain. In doing this, he said, he should not consider himself as acting against his natural sovereign, because he well knew he ought to look for him in the person of the King of France. He explained to me the means whereby my brother might establish himself in Flanders, having possession of Hainault, which extended as far as Brussels. He said the difficulty lay in securing the Cambresis, which is situated betwixt Hainault and Flanders. It would, therefore, be necessary to engage M. d'Ainsi in the business. To this I replied that, as he was his neighbour and friend, it might be better that he should open the matter to him; and I begged he would do so. I next assured him that he might have the most perfect reliance on the gratitude and friendship of my brother, and be certain of receiving as large a share of power and authority as such a service done by a person of his rank merited. Lastly, we agreed upon an interview betwixt my brother and M. de Montigny, the brother of the Count, which was to take place at La Fere, upon my return, when this business should be arranged. During the time I stayed at Mons, I said all I could to confirm the Count in this resolution, in which I found myself seconded by the Countess.

The day of my departure was now arrived, to the great regret of the ladies of Mons, as well as myself. The Countess expressed herself in terms which showed she had conceived the warmest friendship for me, and made me promise to return by way of that city. I presented the Countess with a diamond bracelet, and to the Count I gave a riband and diamond star of considerable value. But these presents, valuable as they were, became more so, in their estimation, as I was the donor.

Of the ladies, none accompanied me from this place, except Madame d'Aurec. She went with me to Namur, where I slept that night, and where she expected to find her husband and the Duc d'Arscot, her brother-in-law, who had been there since the peace betwixt the King of Spain and the States of Flanders. For though they were both of the party of the States, yet the Duc d'Arscot, being an old courtier and having attended King Philip in Flanders and England, could not withdraw himself from Court and the society of the great. The Comte de Lalain, with all his nobles, conducted me two leagues beyond his government, and until he saw Don John's company in the distance advancing to meet me. He then took his leave of me, being unwilling to meet Don John; but M. d'Ainsi stayed with me, as his master, the Bishop of Cambray, was in the Spanish interest.

This gallant company having left me, I was soon after met by Don John of Austria, preceded by a great number of running footmen, and escorted by only twenty or thirty horsemen. He was attended by a number of noblemen, and amongst the rest the Duc d'Arscot, M. d'Aurec, the Marquis de Varenbon, and the younger Balencon, governor, for the King of Spain, of the county of Burgundy. These last two, who are brothers, had ridden post to meet me. Of Don John's household there was only Louis de Gonzago of any rank. He called himself a relation of the Duke of Mantua; the others were mean-looking people, and of no consideration. Don John alighted from his horse to salute me in my litter, which was opened for the purpose. I returned the salute after the French fashion to him, the Duc d'Arscot, and M. d'Aurec. After an exchange of compliments, he mounted his horse, but continued in discourse with me until we reached the city, which was not before it grew dark, as I set off late, the ladies of Mons keeping me as long as they could, amusing themselves with viewing my litter, and requiring an explanation of the different mottoes and devices. However, as the Spaniards excel in preserving good order, Namur appeared with particular advantage, for the streets were well lighted, every house being illuminated, so that the blaze exceeded that of daylight.

Our supper was served to us in our respective apartments, Don John being unwilling, after the fatigue of so long a journey, to incommode us with a banquet. The house in which I was lodged had been newly furnished for the purpose of receiving me. It consisted of a magnificent large salon, with a private apartment, consisting of lodging rooms and closets, furnished in the most costly manner, with furniture of every kind, and hung with the richest tapestry of velvet and satin, divided into compartments by columns of silver embroidery, with knobs of gold, all wrought in the most superb manner. Within these compartments were figures in antique habits, embroidered in gold and silver.

The Cardinal de Lenoncourt, a man of taste and curiosity, being one day in these apartments with the Duc d'Arscot, who, as I have before observed, was an ornament to Don John's Court, remarked to him that this furniture seemed more proper for a great king than a young unmarried prince like Don John. To which the Duc d'Arscot replied that it came to him as a present, having been sent to him by a bashaw belonging to the Grand Seignior, whose son she had made prisoners in a signal victory obtained over the Turks. Don John having sent the bashaw's sons back without ransom, the father, in return, made him a present of a large quantity of gold, silver, and silk stuffs, which he caused to be wrought into tapestry at Milan, where there are curious workmen in this way; and he had the Queen's bedchamber hung with tapestry representing the battle in which he had so gloriously defeated the Turks.

The next morning Don John conducted us to chapel, where we heard mass celebrated after the Spanish manner, with all kinds of music, after which we partook of a banquet prepared by Don John. He and I were seated at a separate table, at a distance of three yards from which stood the great one, of which the honours were done by Madame d'Aurec. At this table the ladies and principal lords took their seats. Don John was served with drink by Louis de Gonzago, kneeling. The tables being removed, the ball was opened, and the dancing continued the whole afternoon. The evening was spent in conversation betwixt Don John and me, who told me I greatly resembled the Queen his mistress, by whom he meant the late Queen my sister, and for whom he professed to have entertained a very high esteem. In short, Don John manifested, by every mark of attention and politeness, as well to me as to my attendants, the very great pleasure he had in receiving me.

The boats which were to convey me upon the Meuse to Liege not all being ready, I was under the necessity of staying another day. The morning was passed as that of the day before. After dinner, we embarked on the river in a very beautiful boat, surrounded by others having on board musicians playing on hautboys, horns, and violins, and landed at an island where Don John had caused a collation to be prepared in a large bower formed with branches of ivy, in which the musicians were placed in small recesses, playing on their instruments during the time of supper. The tables being removed, the dances began, and lasted till it was time to return, which I did in the same boat that conveyed me thither, and which was that provided for my voyage.

The next morning Don John conducted me to the boat, and there took a most polite and courteous leave, charging M. and Madame d'Aurec to see me safe to Huy, the first town belonging to the Bishop of Liege, where I was to sleep. As soon as Don John had gone on shore, M. d'Ainsi, who remained in the boat, and who had the Bishop of Cambray's permission to go to Namur only, took leave of me with many protestations of fidelity and attachment to my brother and myself.

But Fortune, envious of my hitherto prosperous journey, gave me two omens of the sinister events of my return.

The first was the sudden illness which attacked Mademoiselle de Tournon, the daughter of the lady of my bedchamber, a young person, accomplished, with every grace and virtue, and for whom I had the most perfect regard. No sooner had the boat left the shore than this young lady was seized with an alarming disorder, which, from the great pain attending it, caused her to scream in the most doleful manner. The physicians attributed the cause to spasms of the heart, which, notwithstanding the utmost exertions of their skill, carried her off a few days after my arrival at Liege. As the history of this young lady is remarkable, I shall relate it in my next letter.

The other omen was what happened to us at Huy, immediately upon our arrival there. This town is built on the declivity of a mountain, at the foot of which runs the river Meuse. As we were about to land, there fell a torrent of rain, which, coming down the steep sides of the mountain, swelled the river instantly to such a degree that we had only time to leap out of the boat and run to the top, the flood reaching the very highest street, next to where I was to lodge. There we were forced to put up with such accommodation as could be procured in the house, as it was impossible to remove the smallest article of our baggage from the boats, or even to stir out of the house we were in, the whole city being under water. However, the town was as suddenly relieved from this calamity as it had been afflicted with it, for, on the next morning, the whole inundation had ceased, the waters having run off, and the river being confined within its usual channel.

Leaving Huy, M. and Madame d'Aurec returned to Don John at Namur, and I proceeded, in the boat, to sleep that night at Liege.

LETTER XV.

The City of Liege Described. — Affecting Story of Mademoiselle de Tournon. — Fatal Effects of Suppressed Anguish of Mind.

The Bishop of Liege, who is the sovereign of the city and province, received me with all the cordiality and respect that could be expected from a personage of his dignity and great accomplishments. He was, indeed, a nobleman endowed with singular prudence and virtue, agreeable in his person and conversation, gracious and magnificent in his carriage and behaviour, to which I may add that he spoke the French language perfectly.

He was constantly attended by his chapter, with several of his canons, who are all sons of dukes, counts, or great German lords. The bishopric is itself a sovereign State, which brings in a considerable revenue, and includes a number of fine cities. The bishop is chosen from amongst the canons, who must be of noble descent, and resident one year. The city is larger than Lyons, and much resembles it, having the Meuse running through it. The houses in which the canons reside have the appearance of noble palaces.

The streets of the city are regular and spacious, the houses of the citizens well built, the squares large, and ornamented with curious fountains. The churches appear as if raised entirely of marble, of which there are considerable quarries in the neighbourhood; they are all of them ornamented with beautiful clocks, and exhibit a variety of moving figures.

The Bishop received me as I landed from the boat, and conducted me to his magnificent residence, ornamented with delicious fountains and gardens, set off with galleries, all painted, superbly gilt, and enriched with marble, beyond description.

The spring which affords the waters of Spa being distant no more than three or four leagues from the city of Liege, and there being only a village, consisting of three or four small houses, on the spot, the Princesse de Roche-sur-Yon was advised by her physicians to stay at Liege and have the waters brought to her, which they assured her would have equal efficacy, if taken after sunset and before sunrise, as if drunk at the spring. I was well pleased that she resolved to follow the advice of the doctors, as we were more comfortably lodged and had an agreeable society; for, besides his Grace (so the bishop is styled, as a king is addressed his Majesty, and a prince his Highness), the news of my arrival being spread about, many lords and ladies came from Germany to visit me. Amongst these was the Countess d'Aremberg, who had the honour to accompany Queen Elizabeth to Mezieres, to which place she came to marry King Charles my brother, a lady very high in the estimation of the Empress, the Emperor, and all the princes in Christendom. With her came her sister the Landgravine, Madame d'Aremberg her daughter, M. d'Aremberg her son, a gallant and accomplished nobleman, the perfect image of his father, who brought the Spanish succours to King Charles my brother, and returned with great honour and additional reputation. This meeting, so honourable to me, and so much to my satisfaction, was damped by the grief and concern occasioned by the loss of Mademoiselle de Tournon, whose story, being of a singular nature, I shall now relate to you, agreeably to the promise I made in my last letter.

I must begin with observing to you that Madame de Tournon, at this time lady of my bedchamber, had several daughters, the eldest of whom married M. de Balencon, governor, for the King of Spain, in the county of Burgundy. This daughter, upon her marriage, had solicited her mother to admit of her taking her sister, the young lady whose story I am now about to relate, to live with her, as she was going to a country strange to her, and wherein she had no relations. To this her mother consented; and the young lady, being universally admired for her modesty and graceful accomplishments, for which she certainly deserved admiration, attracted the notice of the Marquis de Varenbon. The Marquis, as I before mentioned, is the brother of M. de Balencon, and was intended for the Church; but, being violently enamoured of Mademoiselle de Tournon (whom, as he lived in the same house, he had frequent opportunities of seeing), he now begged his brother's permission to marry her, not having yet taken orders. The young lady's family, to whom he had likewise communicated his wish, readily gave their consent, but his brother refused his, strongly advising him to change his resolution and put on the gown.

Thus were matters situated when her mother, Madame de Tournon, a virtuous and pious lady, thinking she had cause to be offended, ordered her daughter to leave the house of her sister, Madame de Balencon, and come to her. The mother, a woman of a violent spirit, not considering that her daughter was grown up and merited a mild treatment, was continually scolding the poor young lady, so that she was for ever with tears in her eyes. Still, there was nothing to blame in the young girl's conduct, but such was the severity of the mother's disposition. The daughter, as you may well suppose, wished to be from under the mother's tyrannical government, and was accordingly delighted with the thoughts of attending me in this journey to Flanders, hoping, as it happened, that she should meet the Marquis de Varenbon somewhere on the road, and that, as he had now abandoned all thoughts of the Church, he would renew his proposal of marriage, and take her from her mother.

I have before mentioned that the Marquis de Varenbon and the younger Balencon joined us at Namur. Young Balencon, who was far from being so agreeable as his brother, addressed himself to the young lady, but the Marquis, during the whole time we stayed at Namur, paid not the least attention to her, and seemed as if he had never been acquainted with her.

The resentment, grief, and disappointment occasioned by a behaviour so slighting and unnatural was necessarily stifled in her breast, as decorum and her sex's pride obliged her to appear as if she disregarded it; but when, after taking leave, all of them left the boat, the anguish of her mind, which she had hitherto suppressed, could no longer be restrained, and, labouring for vent, it stopped her respiration, and forced from her those lamentable outcries which I have already spoken of. Her youth combated for eight days with this uncommon disorder, but at the expiration of that time she died, to the great grief of her mother, as well as myself. I say of her mother, for, though she was so rigidly severe over this daughter, she tenderly loved her.

The funeral of this unfortunate young lady was solemnised with all proper ceremonies, and conducted in the most honourable manner, as she was descended from a great family, allied to the Queen my mother. When the day of interment arrived, four of my gentlemen were appointed bearers, one of whom was named La Boessiere. This man had entertained a secret passion for her, which he never durst declare on account of the inferiority of his family and station. He was now destined to bear the remains of her, dead, for whom he had long been dying, and was now as near dying for her loss as he had before been for her love. The melancholy procession was marching slowly, along, when it was met by the Marquis de Varenbon, who had been the sole occasion of it. We had not left Namur long when the Marquis reflected upon his cruel behaviour towards this unhappy young lady; and his passion (wonderful to relate) being revived by the absence of her who inspired it, though scarcely alive while she was present, he had resolved to come and ask her of her mother in marriage. He made no doubt, perhaps, of success, as he seldom failed in enterprises of love; witness the great lady he has since obtained for a wife, in opposition to the will of her family. He might, besides, have flattered himself that he should easily have gained a pardon from her by whom he was beloved, according to the Italian proverb, "Che la forza d'amore non riguarda al delitto" (Lovers are not criminal in the estimation of one another). Accordingly, the Marquis solicited Don John to be despatched to me on some errand, and arrived, as I said before, at the very instant the corpse of this ill-fated young lady was being borne to the grave. He was stopped by the crowd occasioned by this solemn procession. He contemplates it for some time. He observes a long train of persons in mourning, and remarks the coffin to be covered with a white pall, and that there are chaplets of flowers laid upon the coffin. He inquires whose funeral it is. The answer he receives is, that it is the funeral of a young lady. Unfortunately for him, this reply fails to satisfy his curiosity. He makes up to one who led the procession, and eagerly asks the name of the young lady they are proceeding to bury. When, oh, fatal answer! Love, willing to avenge the victim of his ingratitude and neglect, suggests a reply which had nearly deprived him of life. He no sooner hears the name of Mademoiselle de Tournon pronounced than he falls from his horse in a swoon. He is taken up for dead, and conveyed to the nearest house, where he lies for a time insensible; his soul, no doubt, leaving his body to obtain pardon from her whom he had hastened to a premature grave, to return to taste the bitterness of death a second time.

Having performed the last offices to the remains of this poor young lady, I was unwilling to discompose the gaiety of the society assembled here on my account by any show of grief. Accordingly, I joined the Bishop, or, as he is called, his Grace, and his canons, in their entertainments at different houses, and in gardens, of which the city and its neighbourhood afforded a variety. I was every morning attended by a numerous company to the garden, in which I drank the waters, the exercise of walking being recommended to be used with them. As the physician who advised me to take them was my own brother, they did not fail of their effect with me; and for these six or seven years which are gone over my head since I drank them, I have been free from any complaint of erysipelas on my arm. From this garden we usually proceeded to the place where we were invited to dinner. After dinner we were amused with a ball; from the ball we went to some convent, where we heard vespers; from vespers to supper, and that over, we had another ball, or music on the river.

LETTER XVI.

Queen Marguerite, on Her Return from Liege, Is in Danger of Being Made a
Prisoner. — She Arrives, after Some Narrow Escapes, at La Fere.

In this manner we passed the six weeks, which is the usual time for taking these waters, at the expiration of which the Princesse de Roche-sur-Yon was desirous to return to France; but Madame d'Aurec, who just then returned to us from Namur, on her way to rejoin her husband in Lorraine, brought us news of an extraordinary change of affairs in that town and province since we had passed through it.

It appeared from this lady's account that, on the very day we left Namur, Don John, after quitting the boat, mounted his horse under pretence of taking the diversion of hunting, and, as he passed the gate of the castle of Namur, expressed a desire of seeing it; that, having entered, he took possession of it, notwithstanding he held it for the States, agreeably to a convention. Don John, moreover, arrested the persons of the Duc d'Arscot and M. d'Aurec, and also made Madame d'Aurec a prisoner. After some remonstrances and entreaties, he had set her husband and brother-in-law at liberty, but detained her as a hostage for them. In consequence of these measures, the whole country was in arms. The province of Namur was divided into three parties: the first whereof was that of the States, or the Catholic party of Flanders; the second that of the Prince of Orange and the Huguenots; the third, the Spanish party, of which Don John was the head.

By letters which I received just at this time from my brother, through the hands of a gentleman named Lescar, I found I was in great danger of falling into the hands of one or other of these parties.

These letters informed me that, since my departure from Court, God had dealt favourably with my brother, and enabled him to acquit himself of the command of the army confided to him, greatly to the benefit of the King's service; so that he had taken all the towns and driven the Huguenots out of the provinces, agreeably to the design for which the army was raised; that he had returned to the Court at Poitiers, where the King stayed during the siege of Brouage, to be near to M. de Mayenne, in order to afford him whatever succours he stood in need of; that, as the Court is a Proteus, forever putting on a new face, he had found it entirely changed, so that he had been no more considered than if he had done the King no service whatever; and that Bussi, who had been so graciously looked upon before and during this last war, had done great personal service, and had lost a brother at the storming of Issoire, was very coolly received, and even as maliciously persecuted as in the time of Le Guast; in consequence of which either he or Bussi experienced some indignity or other. He further mentioned that the King's favourites had been practising with his most faithful servants, Maugiron, La Valette, Mauldon, and Hivarrot, and several other good and trusty men, to desert him, and enter into the King's service; and, lastly, that the King had repented of giving me leave to go to Flanders, and that, to counteract my brother, a plan was laid to intercept me on my return, either by the Spaniards, for which purpose they had been told that I had treated for delivering up the country to him, or by the Huguenots, in revenge of the war my brother had carried on against them, after having formerly assisted them.

This intelligence required to be well considered, as there seemed to be an utter impossibility of avoiding both parties. I had, however, the pleasure to think that two of the principal persons of my company stood well with either one or another party. The Cardinal de Lenoncourt had been thought to favour the Huguenot party, and M. Descarts, brother to the Bishop of Lisieux, was supposed to have the Spanish interest at heart. I communicated our difficult situation to the Princesse de Roche-sur-Yon and Madame de Tournon, who, considering that we could not reach La Fere in less than five or six days, answered me, with tears in their eyes, that God only had it in his power to preserve us, that I should recommend myself to his protection, and then follow such measures as should seem advisable. They observed that, as one of them was in a weak state of health, and the other advanced in years, I might affect to make short journeys on their account, and they would put up with every inconvenience to extricate me from the danger I was in.

I next consulted with the Bishop of Liege, who most certainly acted towards me like a father, and gave directions to the grand master of his household to attend me with his horses as far as I should think proper. As it was necessary that we should have a passport from the Prince of Orange, I sent Mondoucet to him to obtain one, as he was acquainted with the Prince and was known to favour his religion. Mondoucet did not return, and I believe I might have waited for him until this time to no purpose. I was advised by the Cardinal de Lenoncourt and my first esquire, the Chevalier Salviati, who were of the same party, not to stir without a passport; but, as I suspected a plan was laid to entrap me, I resolved to set out the next morning.

They now saw that this pretence was insufficient to detain me; accordingly, the Chevalier Salviati prevailed with my treasurer, who was secretly a Huguenot, to declare he had not money enough in his hands to discharge the expenses we had incurred at Liege, and that, in consequence, my horses were detained. I afterwards discovered that this was false, for, on my arrival at La Fere, I called for his accounts, and found he had then a balance in his hands which would have enabled him to pay, the expenses of my family for six or seven weeks. The Princesse de Roche-sur-Yon, incensed at the affront put upon me, and seeing the danger I incurred by staying, advanced the money that was required, to their great confusion; and I took my leave of his Grace the Bishop, presenting him with a diamond worth three thousand crowns, and giving his domestics gold chains and rings. Having thus taken our leave, we proceeded to Huy, without any other passport than God's good providence.

This town, as I observed before, belongs to the Bishop of Liege, but was now in a state of tumult and confusion, on account of the general revolt of the Low Countries, the townsmen taking part with the Netherlanders, notwithstanding the bishopric was a neutral

State. On this account they paid no respect to the grand master of the Bishop's household, who accompanied us, but, knowing Don John had taken the castle of Namur in order, as they supposed, to intercept me on my return, these brutal people, as soon as I had got into my quarters, rang the alarm-bell, drew up their artillery, placed chains across the streets, and kept us thus confined and separated the whole night, giving us no opportunity to expostulate with them on such conduct. In the morning we were suffered to leave the town without further molestation, and the streets we passed through were lined with armed men.

From there we proceeded to Dinant, where we intended to sleep; but, unfortunately for us, the townspeople had on that day chosen their burghermasters, a kind of officers like the consuls in Gascony and France. In consequence of this election, it was a day of tumult, riot, and debauchery; every one in the town was drunk, no magistrate was acknowledged. In a word, all was in confusion. To render our situation still worse, the grand master of the Bishop's household had formerly done the town some ill office, and was considered as its enemy. The people of the town, when in their sober senses, were inclined to favour the party of the States, but under the influence of Bacchus they paid no regard to any party, not even to themselves.

As soon as I had reached the suburbs, they were alarmed at the number of my company, quitted the bottle and glass to take up their arms, and immediately shut the gates against me. I had sent a gentleman before me, with my harbinger and quartermasters, to beg the magistrates to admit me to stay one night in the town, but I found my officers had been put under an arrest. They bawled out to us from within, to tell us their situation, but could not make themselves heard. At length I raised myself up in my litter, and, taking off my mask, made a sign to a townsman nearest me, of the best appearance, that I was desirous to speak with him. As soon as he drew near me, I begged him to call out for silence, which being with some difficulty obtained, I represented to him who I was, and the occasion of my journey; that it was far from my intention to do them harm; but, to prevent any suspicions of the kind, I only begged to be admitted to go into their city with my women, and as few others of my attendants as they thought proper, and that we might be permitted to stay there for one night, whilst the rest of my company remained within the suburbs.

They agreed to this proposal, and opened their gates for my admission. I then entered the city with the principal persons of my company, and the grand master of the Bishop's household. This reverend personage, who was eighty years of age, and wore a beard as white as snow, which reached down to his girdle, this venerable old man, I say, was no sooner recognised by the drunken and armed rabble than he was accosted with the grossest abuse, and it was with difficulty they were restrained from laying violent hands upon him. At length I got him into my lodgings, but the mob fired at the house, the walls of which were only of plaster. Upon being thus attacked, I inquired for the master of the house, who, fortunately, was within. I entreated him to speak from the window, to some one without, to obtain permission for my being heard. I had some difficulty to get him to venture doing so. At length, after much bawling from the window, the burghermasters came to speak to me, but were so drunk that they scarcely knew what they said. I explained to them that I was entirely ignorant that the grand master of the Bishop's household was a person to whom they had a dislike, and I begged them to consider the consequences of giving offence to a person like me, who was a friend of the principal lords of the States, and I assured them that the Comte de Lalain, in particular, would be greatly displeased when he should hear how I had been received there.

The name of the Comte de Lalain produced an instant effect, much more than if I had mentioned all the sovereign princes I was related to. The principal person amongst them asked me, with some hesitation and stammering, if I was really a particular friend of the Count's. Perceiving that to claim kindred with the Count would do me more service than being related to all the Powers in Christendom, I answered that I was both a friend and a relation. They then made me many apologies and conges, stretching forth their hands in token of friendship; in short, they now behaved with as much civility as before with rudeness.

They begged my pardon for what had happened, and promised that the good old man, the grand master of the Bishop's household, should be no more insulted, but be suffered to leave the city quietly, the next morning, with me.

As soon as morning came, and while I was preparing to go to hear mass, there arrived the King's agent to Don John, named Du Bois, a man much attached to the Spanish interest. He informed me that he had received orders from the King my brother to conduct me in safety on my return. He said that he had prevailed on Don John to permit Barlemont to escort me to Namur with a troop of cavalry, and begged me to obtain leave of the citizens to admit Barlemont and his troop to enter the town that; they might receive my orders.

Thus had they concerted a double plot; the one to get possession of the town, the other of my person. I saw through the whole design, and consulted with the Cardinal de Lenoncourt, communicating to him my suspicions. The Cardinal was as unwilling to fall into the hands of the Spaniards as I could be; he therefore thought it advisable to acquaint the townspeople with the plot, and make our escape from the city by another road, in order to avoid meeting Barlemont's troop. It was agreed betwixt us that the Cardinal should keep Du Bois in discourse, whilst I consulted the principal citizens in another apartment.

Accordingly, I assembled as many as I could, to whom I represented that if they admitted Barlemont and his troop within the town, he would most certainly take possession of it for Don John. I gave it as my advice to make a show of defence, to declare they would not be taken by surprise, and to offer to admit Barlemont, and no one else, within their gates. They resolved to act according to my counsel, and offered to serve me at the hazard of their lives. They promised to procure me a guide, who should conduct me by a road by following which I should put the river betwixt me and Don John's forces, whereby I should be out of his reach, and could be lodged in houses and towns which were in the interest of the States only.

This point being settled, I despatched them to give admission to M. de Barlemont, who, as soon as he entered within the gates, begged hard that his troop might come in likewise. Hereupon, the citizens flew into a violent rage, and were near putting him to death. They told him that if he did not order his men out of sight of the town, they would fire upon them with their great guns. This was done with design to give me time to leave the town before they could follow in pursuit of me. M. de Barlemont and the agent, Du Bois, used every argument they could devise to persuade me to go to Namur, where they said Don John waited to receive me.

I appeared to give way to their persuasions, and, after hearing mass and taking a hasty dinner, I left my lodgings, escorted by two or three hundred armed citizens, some of them engaging Barlemont and Du Bois in conversation. We all took the way to the gate which opens to the river, and directly opposite to that leading to Namur. Du Bois and his colleague told me I was not going the right way, but I continued talking, and as if I did not hear them. But when we reached the gate I hastened into the boat, and my people after me. M. de Barlemont and the agent Du Bois, calling out to me from the bank, told me I was doing very wrong and acting directly contrary to the King's intention, who had directed that I should return by way of Namur.

In spite of all their remonstrances we crossed the river with all possible expedition, and, during the two or three crossings which were necessary to convey over the litters and horses, the citizens, to give me the more time to escape, were debating with Barlemont and Du Bois concerning a number of grievances and complaints, telling them, in their coarse language, that Don John had broken the peace and falsified his engagements with the States; and they even re-hearsed the old quarrel of the death of Egmont, and, lastly, declared that if the troop made its appearance before their walls again, they would fire upon it with their artillery.

I had by this means sufficient time to reach a secure distance, and was, by the help of God and the assistance of my guide, out of all apprehensions of danger from Barlemont and his troop.

I intended to lodge that night in a strong castle, called Fleurines, which belonged to a gentleman of the party of the States, whom I had seen with the Comte de Lalain. Unfortunately for me, the gentleman was absent, and his lady only was in the castle. The court-yard being open, we entered it, which put the lady into such a fright that she ordered the bridge to be drawn up, and fled to the strong tower. — [In the old French original, 'dongeon', whence we have 'duugeon'.] — Nothing we could say would induce her to give us entrance. In the meantime, three hundred gentlemen, whom Don John had sent off to intercept our passage, and take possession of the castle of Fleurines; judging that I should take up my quarters there, made their appearance upon an eminence, at the distance of about a thousand yards. They, seeing our carriages in the courtyard, and supposing that we ourselves had taken to the strong tower, resolved to stay where they were that night, hoping to intercept me the next morning.

In this cruel situation were we placed, in a courtyard surrounded by a wall by no means strong, and shut up by a gate equally as weak and as capable of being forced, remonstrating from time to time with the lady, who was deaf to all our prayers and entreaties.

Through God's mercy, her husband, M. de Fleurines, himself appeared just as night approached. We then gained instant admission, and the lady was greatly reprimanded by her husband for her incivility and indiscreet behaviour. This gentleman had been sent by the Comte de Lalain, with directions to conduct me through the several towns belonging to the States, the Count himself not being able to leave the army of the States, of which he had the chief command, to accompany me.

This was as favourable a circumstance for me as I could wish; for, M. de Fleurines offering to accompany me into France, the towns we had to pass through being of the party of the States, we were everywhere quietly and honourably received. I had only the mortification of not being able to visit Mons, agreeably to my promise made to the Comtesse de Lalain, not passing nearer to it than Nivelle, seven long leagues distant from it. The Count being at Antwerp, and the war being hottest in the neighbourhood of Mons, I thus was prevented seeing either of them on my return. I could only write to the Countess by a servant of the gentleman who was now my conductor. As soon as she learned I was at Nivelle, she sent some gentlemen, natives of the part of Flanders I was in, with a strong injunction to see me safe on the frontier of France.

I had to pass through the Cambresis, partly in favour of Spain and partly of the States. Accordingly, I set out with these gentlemen, to lodge at Cateau Cambresis. There they took leave of me, in order to return to Mons, and by them I sent the Countess a gown of mine, which had been greatly admired by her when I wore it at Mons; it was of black satin, curiously embroidered, and cost nine hundred crowns.

When I arrived at Cateau-Cambresis, I had intelligence sent me that a party of the Huguenot troops had a design to attack me on the frontiers of Flanders and France. This intelligence I communicated to a few only of my company, and prepared to set off an hour before daybreak. When I sent for my litters and horses, I found much such a kind of delay from the Chevalier Salviati as I had before experienced at Liege, and suspecting it was done designedly, I left my litter behind, and mounted on horseback, with such of my attendants as were ready to follow me. By this means, with God's assistance, I escaped being waylaid by my enemies, and reached Catelet at ten in the morning. From there I went to my house at La Fere, where I intended to reside until I learned that peace was concluded upon.

At La Fere I found a messenger in waiting from my brother, who had orders to return with all expedition, as soon as I arrived, and inform him of it. My brother wrote me word, by that messenger, that peace was concluded, and the King returned to Paris; that, as to himself, his situation was rather worse than better; that he and his people were daily receiving some affront or other, and continual quarrels were excited betwixt the King's favourites and Bussi and my brother's principal attendants. This, he added, had made him impatient for my return, that he might come and visit me.

I sent his messenger back, and, immediately after, my brother sent Bussi and all his household to Angers, and, taking with him fifteen or twenty attendants, he rode post to me at La Fere. It was a great satisfaction to me to see one whom I so tenderly loved and greatly honoured, once more. I consider it amongst the greatest felicities I ever enjoyed, and, accordingly, it became my chief study to make his residence here agreeable to him. He himself seemed delighted with this change of situation, and would willingly have continued in it longer had not the noble generosity of his mind called him forth to great achievements. The quiet of our Court,

when compared with that he had just left, affected him so powerful-
ly that he could not but express the satisfaction he felt by frequently
exclaiming, "Oh, Queen! how happy I am with you. My God! your
society is a paradise wherein I enjoy every delight, and I seem to
have lately escaped from hell, with all its furies and tortures!"

LETTER XVII.

Good Effects of Queen Marguerite's Negotiations in Flanders.—She Obtains
Leave to Go to the King of Navarre Her Husband, but Her Journey Is
Delayed.—Court Intrigues and Plots.—The Duc d'Alencon Again Put under
Arrest.

We passed nearly two months together, which appeared to us only as so many days. I gave him an account of what I had done for him in Flanders, and the state in which I had left the business. He approved of the interview with the Comte de Lalain's brother in order to settle the plan of operations and exchange assurances. Accordingly, the Comte de Montigny arrived, with four or five other leading men of the county of Hainault. One of these was charged with a letter from M. d'Ainsi, offering his services to my brother, and assuring him of the citadel of Cambray. M. de Montigny delivered his brother's declaration and engagement to give up the counties of Hainault and Artois, which included a number of fine cities. These offers made and accepted, my brother dismissed them with presents of gold medals, bearing his and my effigies, and every assurance of his future favour; and they returned to prepare everything for his coming. In the meanwhile my brother considered on the necessary measures to be used for raising a sufficient force, for which purpose he returned to the King, to prevail with him to assist him in this enterprise.

As I was anxious to go to Gascony, I made ready for the journey, and set off for Paris, my brother meeting me at the distance of one day's journey.

At St. Denis I was met by the King, the Queen my mother, Queen Louise, and the whole Court. It was at St. Denis that I was to stop and dine, and there it was that I had the honour of the meeting I have just mentioned.

I was received very graciously, and most sumptuously entertained. I was made to recount the particulars of my triumphant journey to Liege, and perilous return. The magnificent entertainments I had received excited their admiration, and they rejoiced at my narrow escapes. With such conversation I amused the Queen my mother and the rest of the company in her coach, on our way to Paris, where, supper and the ball being ended, I took an opportunity, when I saw the King and the Queen my mother together, to address them.

I expressed my hopes that they would not now oppose my going to the King my husband; that now, by the peace, the chief objection to it was removed, and if I delayed going, in the present situation of affairs, it might be prejudicial and discreditable to me. Both of them approved of my request, and commended my resolution. The Queen my mother added that she would accompany me on my journey, as it would be for the King's service that she did so. She said the King must furnish me with the necessary means for the journey, to which he readily assented. I thought this a proper time to settle everything, and prevent another journey to Court, which would be no longer pleasing after my brother left it, who was now pressing his expedition to Flanders with all haste. I therefore begged the Queen my mother to recollect the promise she had made my brother and me as soon as peace was agreed upon, which was that, before my departure for Gascony, I should have my marriage portion assigned to me in lands. She said that she recollected it well, and the King thought it very reasonable, and promised that it should be done. I entreated that it might be concluded speedily, as I wished to set off, with their permission, at the beginning of the next month. This, too, was granted me, but granted after the mode of the Court; that is to say, notwithstanding my constant solicitations, instead of despatch, I experienced only delay; and thus it continued for five or six months in negotiation.

My brother met with the like treatment, though he was continually urging the necessity for his setting out for Flanders, and representing that his expedition was for the glory and advantage of

France,—for its glory, as such an enterprise would, like Piedmont, prove a school of war for the young nobility, wherein future Montlucs, Brissacs, Termes, and Bellegardes would be bred, all of them instructed in these wars, and afterwards, as field-marshals, of the greatest service to their country; and it would be for the advantage of France, as it would prevent civil wars; for Flanders would then be no longer a country wherein such discontented spirits as aimed at novelty could assemble to brood over their malice and hatch plots for the disturbance of their native land.

These representations, which were both reasonable and consonant with truth, had no weight when put into the scale against the envy excited by this advancement of my brother's fortune. Accordingly, every delay was used to hinder him from collecting his forces together, and stop his expedition to Flanders. Bussi and his other dependents were offered a thousand indignities. Every stratagem was tried, by day as well as by night, to pick quarrels with Bussi,—now by Quelus, at another time by Grammont, with the hope that my brother would engage in them. This was unknown to the King; but Maugiron, who had engrossed the King's favour, and who had quitted my brother's service, sought every means to ruin him, as it is usual for those who have given offence to hate the offended party.

Thus did this man take every occasion to brave and insult my brother; and relying upon the countenance and blind affection shown him by the King, had leagued himself with Quelus, Saint-Luc, Saint-Maigrin, Grammont, Mauleon, Hivarrot, and other young men who enjoyed the King's favour. As those who are favourites find a number of followers at Court, these licentious young courtiers thought they might do whatever they pleased. Some new dispute betwixt them and Bussi was constantly starting. Bussi had a degree of courage which knew not how to give way to any one; and my brother, unwilling to give umbrage to the King, and foreseeing that such proceedings would not forward his expedition, to avoid quarrels and, at the same time, to promote his plans, resolved to despatch Bussi to his duchy of Alencon, in order to discipline such troops as he should find there. My brother's amiable qualities excited the jealousy of Maugiron and the rest of his cabal about the King's person, and their dislike for Bussi was not so much on his own account as because he was strongly attached to my brother. The slights and disrespect shown to my brother were remarked by every one at Court; but his prudence, and the patience natural to his disposition, enabled him to put up with their insults, in hopes of finishing the business of his Flemish expedition, which would remove him to a distance from them and their machinations. This persecution was the more mortifying and discreditable as it even extended to his servants, whom they strove to injure by every means they could employ. M. de la Chastre at this time had a law-suit of considerable consequence decided against him, because he had lately attached himself to my brother. At the instance of Maugiron and Saint-Luc, the King was induced to solicit the cause in favour of Madame de Senetaire, their friend. M. de la Chastre, being greatly injured by it, complained to my brother of the injustice done him, with all the concern such a proceeding may be supposed to have occasioned.

About this time Saint-Luc's marriage was celebrated. My brother resolved not to be present at it, and begged of me to join him in the same resolution. The Queen my mother was greatly uneasy on account of the behaviour of these young men, fearing that, if my brother did not join them in this festivity, it might be attended with some bad consequence, especially as the day was likely to produce scenes of revelry and debauch; she, therefore, prevailed on the King to permit her to dine on the wedding-day at St. Maur, and take my brother and me with her. This was the day before Shrove Tuesday; and we returned in the evening, the Queen my mother having well lectured my brother, and made him consent to appear at the ball, in order not to displease the King.

But this rather served to make matters worse than better, for Maugiron and his party began to attack him with such violent speeches as would have offended any one of far less consequence. They said he needed not to have given himself the trouble of dressing, for he was not missed in the afternoon; but now, they supposed, he came at night as the most suitable time; with other allusions to the meanness of his figure and smallness of stature. All this was addressed to the bride, who sat near him, but spoken out on purpose that he might hear it. My brother, perceiving this was purposely said to provoke an answer and occasion his giving offence to the King, removed from his seat full of resentment; and, consulting with M. de la Chastre, he came to the resolution of leaving the Court in a few days on a hunting party. He still thought his absence might stay their malice, and afford him an opportunity the more easily of settling his preparations for the Flemish expedition with the King. He went immediately to the Queen my mother, who was present at the ball, and was extremely sorry to learn what had happened, and imparted her resolution, in his absence, to solicit the King to hasten his expedition to Flanders. M. de Villequier being present, she bade him acquaint the King with my brother's intention of taking the diversion of hunting a few days; which she thought very proper herself, as it would put a stop to the disputes which had arisen betwixt him and the young men, Maugiron, Saint-Luc, Quelus, and the rest.

My brother retired to his apartment, and, considering his leave as granted, gave orders to his domestics to prepare to set off the next morning for St. Germain, where he should hunt the stag for a few days. He directed the grand huntsman to be ready with the hounds, and retired to rest, thinking to withdraw awhile from the intrigues of the Court, and amuse himself with the sports of the field. M. de Villequier, agreeably to the command he had received from the Queen my mother, asked for leave, and obtained it. The King, however, staying in his closet, like Rehoboam, with his council of five or six young men, they suggested suspicions in his mind respecting my brother's departure from Court. In short, they worked upon his fears and apprehensions so greatly, that he took one of the most rash and inconsiderate steps that was ever decided upon in our time; which was to put my brother and all his principal servants under an arrest. This measure was executed with as much indiscretion as it had been resolved upon. The King, under this agitation of mind, late as it was, hastened to the Queen my mother, and seemed as if there was a general alarm and the enemy at the gates, for he exclaimed on seeing her: "How could you, Madame, think of asking me to let my brother go hence? Do you not perceive how dangerous his going will prove to my kingdom? Depend upon it that this hunting is merely a pretence to cover some treacherous design. I am going to put him and his people under an arrest, and have his papers examined. I am sure we shall make some great discoveries."

At the time he said this he had with him the Sieur de Cosse, captain of the guard, and a number of Scottish archers. The Queen my mother, fearing, from the King's haste and trepidation, that some mischief might happen to my brother, begged to go with him. Accordingly, undressed as she was, wrapping herself up in a nightgown, she followed the King to my brother's bedchamber. The King knocked at the door with great violence, ordering it to be immediately opened, for that he was there himself. My brother started up in his bed, awakened by the noise, and, knowing that he had done nothing that he need fear, ordered Cange, his valet de chambre, to open the door. The King entered in a great rage, and asked him when he would have done plotting against him. "But I will show you," said he, "what it is to plot against your sovereign." Hereupon he ordered the archers to take away all the trunks, and turn the valets de chambre out of the room. He searched my brother's bed himself, to see if he could find any papers concealed in it. My brother had that evening received a letter from Madame de Sauves, which he kept in his hand, unwilling that it should be seen. The King endeavoured to force it from him. He refused to part with it, and earnestly entreated the King would not insist upon seeing it. This only excited the King's anxiety the more to have it in his possession, as he now supposed it to be the key to the whole plot, and the very document which would at once bring conviction home to him. At length, the King having got it into his hands, he opened it in the presence of the Queen my mother, and they were both as much confounded, when they read the contents, as Cato was when he obtained a letter from Caesar, in the Senate, which the latter was unwilling to give up; and which Cato, supposing it to contain a conspiracy against the Republic, found to be no other than a love-letter from his own sister.

But the shame of this disappointment served only to increase the King's anger, who, without condescending to make a reply to my brother, when repeatedly asked what he had been accused of, gave him in charge of M. de Cosse and his Scots, commanding them not to admit a single person to speak with him.

It was one o'clock in the morning when my brother was made a prisoner in the manner I have now related. He feared some fatal event might succeed these violent proceedings, and he was under the greatest concern on my account, supposing me to be under a like arrest. He observed M. de Cosse to be much affected by the scene he had been witness to, even to shedding tears. As the archers were in the room he would not venture to enter into discourse with him, but only asked what was become of me. M. de Cosse answered that I remained at full liberty. My brother then said it was a great comfort to him to hear that news; "but," added he, "as I know she loves me so entirely that she would rather be confined with me than have her liberty whilst I was in confinement, I beg you will go to the Queen my mother, and desire her to obtain leave for my sister to be with me." He did so, and it was granted.

The reliance which my brother displayed upon this occasion in the sincerity of my friendship and regard for him conferred so great an obligation in my mind that, though I have received many particular favours since from him, this has always held the foremost place in my grateful remembrance.

By the time he had received permission for my being with him, daylight made its appearance. Seeing this, my brother begged M. de Cosse to send one of his archers to acquaint me with his situation, and beg me to come to him.

LETTER XVIII.

The Brothers Reconciled. — Alencon Restored to His Liberty.

I was ignorant of what had happened to my brother, and when the Scottish archer came into my bedchamber, I was still asleep. He drew the curtains of the bed, and told me, in his broken French, that my brother wished to see me. I stared at the man, half awake as I was, and thought it a dream. After a short pause, and being thoroughly awakened, I asked him if he was not a Scottish archer. He answered me in the affirmative. "What!" cried I, "has my brother no one else to send a message by?" He replied he had not, for all his domestics had been put under an arrest. He then proceeded to relate, as well as he could explain himself, the events of the preceding night, and the leave granted my brother for my being with him during his imprisonment.

The poor fellow, observing me to be much affected by this intelligence, drew near, and whispered me to this purport: "Do not grieve yourself about this matter; I know a way of setting your brother at liberty, and you may depend upon it, that I will do it; but, in that case, I must go off with him." I assured him that he might rely upon being as amply rewarded as he could wish for such assistance, and, huddling on my clothes, I followed him alone to my brother's apartments. In going thither, I had occasion to traverse the whole gallery, which was filled with people, who, at another time, would have pressed forward to pay their respects to me; but, now that Fortune seemed to frown upon me, they all avoided me, or appeared as if they did not see me.

Coming into my brother's apartments, I found him not at all affected by what had happened; for such was the constancy of his mind, that his arrest had wrought no change, and he received me with his usual cheerfulness. He ran to meet me, and taking me in his arms, he said, "Queen! I beg you to dry up your tears; in my present situation, nothing can grieve me so much as to find you under any concern; for my own part, I am so conscious of my innocence and the integrity of my conduct, that I can defy the utmost malice of my enemies. If I should chance to fall the victim of their injustice, my death would prove a more cruel punishment to them than to me, who have courage sufficient to meet it in a just cause. It is not death I fear, because I have tasted sufficiently of the calamities and evils of life, and am ready to leave this world, which I have found only the abode of sorrow; but the circumstance I dread most is, that, not finding me sufficiently guilty to doom me to death, I shall be condemned to a long, solitary imprisonment; though I should even despise their tyranny in that respect, could I but have the assurance of being comforted by your presence."

These words, instead of stopping my tears, only served to make them stream afresh. I answered, sobbing, that my life and fortune were at his devotion; that the power of God alone could prevent me from affording him my assistance under every extremity; that, if he should be transported from that place, and I should be withheld from following him, I would kill myself on the spot.

Changing our discourse, we framed a number of conjectures on what might be the probable cause of the King's angry proceedings against him, but found ourselves at a loss what to assign them to.

Whilst we were discussing this matter the hour came for opening the palace gates, when a simple young man belonging to Bussi presented himself for entrance. Being stopped by the guard and questioned as to whither he was going, he, panic-struck, replied he was going to M. de Bussi, his master. This answer was carried to the King, and gave fresh grounds for suspicion. It seems my brother, supposing he should not be able to go to Flanders for some time, and resolving to send Bussi to his duchy of Alencon as I have already mentioned, had lodged him in the Louvre, that he might be near him to take instructions at every opportunity.

L'Archant, the general of the guard, had received the King's commands to make a search in the Louvre for him and Simier, and put them both under arrest. He entered upon this business with great unwillingness, as he was intimate with Bussi, who was accustomed to call him "father." L'Archant, going to Simier's apartment, arrested him; and though he judged Bussi was there too, yet, being unwilling to find him, he was going away. Bussi, however, who had concealed himself under the bed, as not knowing to whom the orders for his arrest might be given, finding he was to be left there, and sensible that he should be well treated by L'Archant, called out to him, as he was leaving the room, in his droll manner: "What, papa, are you going without me? Don't you think I am as great a rogue as that Simier?"

"Ah, son," replied L'Archant, "I would much rather have lost my arm than have met with you!"

Bussi, being a man devoid of all fear, observed that it was a sign that things went well with him; then, turning to Simier, who stood trembling with fear, he jeered him upon his pusillanimity. L'Archant removed them both, and set a guard over them; and, in the next place, proceeded to arrest M. de la Chastre, whom he took to the Bastille.

Meanwhile M. de l'Oste was appointed to the command of the guard which was set over my brother. This was a good sort of old man, who had been appointed governor to the King my husband, and loved me as if I had been his own child. Sensible of the injustice done to my brother and me, and lamenting the bad counsel by which the King was guided, and being, moreover, willing to serve us, he resolved to deliver my brother from arrest. In order to make his intention known to us he ordered the Scottish archers to wait on the stairs without, keeping only, two whom he could trust in the room. Then taking me aside, he said:

"There is not a good Frenchman living who does not bleed at his heart to see what we see. I have served the King your father, and I am ready to lay down my life to serve his children. I expect to have the guard of the Prince your brother, wherever he shall chance to be confined; and, depend upon it, at the hazard of my life, I will restore him to his liberty. But," added he, "that no suspicions may arise that such is my design, it will be proper that we be not seen together in conversation; however, you may, rely upon my word."

This afforded me great consolation; and, assuming a degree of courage hereupon, I observed to my brother that we ought not to remain there without knowing for what reason we were detained, as if we were in the Inquisition; and that to treat us in such a manner was to consider us as persons of no account. I then begged M. de l'Oste to entreat the King, in our name, if the Queen our mother was not permitted to come to us, to send some one to acquaint us with the crime for which we were kept in confinement.

M. de Combaut, who was at the head of the young counsellors, was accordingly sent to us; and he, with a great deal of gravity, informed us that he came from the King to inquire what it was we wished to communicate to his Majesty. We answered that we wished to speak to some one near the King's person, in order to our being informed what we were kept in confinement for, as we were unable to assign any reason for it ourselves. He answered, with great solemnity, that we ought not to ask of God or the King reasons for what they did; as all their actions emanated from wisdom and justice. We replied that we were not persons to be treated like those shut up in the Inquisition, who are left to guess at the cause of their being there.

We could obtain from him, after all we said, no other satisfaction than his promise to interest himself in our behalf, and to do us all the service in his power. At this my brother broke out into a fit of laughter; but I confess I was too much alarmed to treat his message with such indifference, and could scarcely, refrain from talking to this messenger as he deserved.

Whilst he was making his report to the King, the Queen my mother kept her chamber, being under great concern, as may well be supposed, to witness such proceedings. She plainly foresaw, in her prudence, that these excesses would end fatally, should the mildness of my brother's disposition, and his regard for the welfare of the State, be once wearied out with submitting to such repeated acts of injustice. She therefore sent for the senior members of the Council, the chancellor, princes, nobles, and marshals of France, who all were greatly scandalised at the bad counsel which had been given to the King, and told the Queen my mother that she ought to remonstrate with the King upon the injustice of his proceedings. They observed that what had been done could not now be recalled, but matters might yet be set upon a right footing. The Queen my mother hereupon went to the King, followed by these counsellors, and represented to him the ill consequences which might proceed from the steps he had taken.

The King's eyes were by this time opened, and he saw that he had been ill advised. He therefore begged the Queen my mother to set things to rights, and to prevail on my brother to forget all that had happened, and to bear no resentment against these young men, but to make up the breach betwixt Bussi and Quelus.

Things being thus set to rights again, the guard which had been placed over my brother was dismissed, and the Queen my mother, coming to his apartment, told him he ought to return thanks to God for his deliverance, for that there had been a moment when even she herself despaired of saving his life; that since he must now have discovered that the King's temper of mind was such that he took the alarm at the very imagination of danger, and that, when once he was resolved upon a measure, no advice that she or any other could give would prevent him from putting it into execution, she would recommend it to him to submit himself to the King's pleasure in everything, in order to prevent the like in future; and, for the present, to take the earliest opportunity of seeing the King, and to appear as if he thought no more about the past.

We replied that we were both of us sensible of God's great mercy in delivering us from the injustice of our enemies, and that, next to God, our greatest obligation was to her; but that my brother's rank did not admit of his being put in confinement without cause, and released from it again without the formality of an acknowledgment. Upon this, the Queen observed that it was not in the power even of God himself to undo what had been done; that what could be effected to save his honour, and give him satisfaction for the irregularity of the arrest, should have place. My brother, therefore, she observed, ought to strive to mollify the King by addressing him with expressions of regard to his person and attachment to his service; and, in the meantime, use his influence over Bussi to reconcile him to Quelus, and to end all disputes betwixt them. She then declared that the principal motive for putting my brother and his servants under arrest was to prevent the combat for which old Bussi, the brave father of a brave son, had solicited the King's leave, wherein he proposed to be his son's second, whilst the father of

Quelus was to be his. These four had agreed in this way to deter-mine the matter in dispute, and give the Court no further disturb-ance.

My brother now engaged himself to the Queen that, as Bussi would see he could not be permitted to decide his quarrel by com-bat, he should, in order to deliver himself from his arrest, do as she had commanded.

The Queen my mother, going down to the King, prevailed with him to restore my brother to liberty with every honour. In order to which the King came to her apartment, followed by the princes, noblemen, and other members of the Council, and sent for us by M. de Villequier. As we went along we found all the rooms crowded with people, who, with tears in their eyes, blessed God for our de-liverance. Coming into the apartments of the Queen my mother, we found the King attended as I before related. The King desired my brother not to take anything ill that had been done, as the motive for it was his concern for the good of his kingdom, and not any bad intention towards himself. My brother replied that he had, as he ought, devoted his life to his service, and, therefore, was governed by his pleasure; but that he most humbly begged him to consider that his fidelity and attachment did not merit the return he had met with; that, notwithstanding, he should impute it entirely to his own ill-fortune, and should be perfectly satisfied if the King acknowl-edged his innocence. Hereupon the King said that he entertained not the least doubt of his innocence, and only desired him to believe he held the same place in his esteem he ever had. The Queen my mother then, taking both of them by the hand, made them embrace each other.

Afterwards the King commanded Bussi to be brought forth, to make a reconciliation betwixt him and Quelus, giving orders, at the same time, for the release of Simier and M. de la Chastre. Bussi com-ing into the room with his usual grace, the King told him he must be reconciled with Quelus, and forbade him to say a word more con-cerning their quarrel. He then commanded them to embrace. "Sire," said Bussi, "if it is your pleasure that we kiss and are friends again, I am ready to obey your command;" then, putting himself in the atti-tude of Pantaloon, he went up to Queus and gave him a hug, which set all present in a titter, notwithstanding they had been seriously affected by the scene which had passed just before.

Many persons of discretion thought what had been done was too slight a reparation for the injuries my brother had received. When all was over, the King and the Queen my mother, coming up to me, said it would be incumbent on me to use my utmost endeavours to prevent my brother from calling to mind anything past which should make him swerve from the duty and affection he owed the King. I replied that my brother was so prudent, and so strongly attached to the King's service, that he needed no admonition on that head from me or any one else; and that, with respect to myself, I had never given him any other advice than to conform himself to the King's pleasure and the duty he owed him.

LETTER XIX.

The Duc d'Alencon Makes His Escape from Court. — Queen Marguerite's
Fidelity Put to a Severe Trial.

It was now three o'clock in the afternoon, and no one present had yet dined. The Queen my mother was desirous that we should eat together, and, after dinner, she ordered my brother and me to change our dress (as the clothes we had on were suitable only to our late melancholy situation) and come to the King's supper and ball. We complied with her orders as far as a change of dress, but our countenances still retained the impressions of grief and resentment which we inwardly felt.

I must inform you that when the tragi-comedy I have given you an account of was over, the Queen my mother turned round to the Chevalier de Seurre, whom she recommended to my brother to sleep in his bedchamber, and in whose conversation she sometimes took delight because he was a man of some humour, but rather inclined to be cynical.

"Well," said she, "M. de Seurre, what do you think of all this?"

"Madame, I think there is too much of it for earnest, and not enough for jest."

Then addressing himself to me, he said, but not loud enough for the Queen to hear him: "I do not believe all is over yet; I am very much mistaken if this young man" (meaning my brother) "rests satisfied with this." This day having passed in the manner before related, the wound being only skinned over and far from healed, the young men about the King's person set themselves to operate in order to break it out afresh.

These persons, judging of my brother by themselves, and not having sufficient experience to know the power of duty over the minds of personages of exalted rank and high birth, persuaded the King, still connecting his case with their own, that it was impossible my brother should ever forgive the affront he had received, and not seek to avenge himself with the first opportunity. The King, forgetting the ill-judged steps these young men had so lately induced him to take, hereupon receives this new impression, and gives orders to the officers of the guard to keep strict watch at the gates that his brother go not out, and that his people be made to leave the Louvre every evening, except such of them as usually slept in his bedchamber or wardrobe.

My brother, seeing himself thus exposed to the caprices of these headstrong young fellows, who led the King according to their own fancies, and fearing something worse might happen than what he had yet experienced, at the end of three days, during which time he laboured under apprehensions of this kind, came to a determination to leave the Court, and never more return to it, but retire to his principality and make preparations with all haste for his expedition to Flanders. He communicated his design to me, and I approved of it, as I considered he had no other view in it than providing for his own safety, and that neither the King nor his government were likely to sustain any injury by it.

When we consulted upon the means of its accomplishment, we could find no other than his descending from my window, which was on the second story and opened to the ditch, for the gates were so closely watched that it was impossible to pass them, the face of every one going out of the Louvre being curiously examined. He begged of me, therefore, to procure for him a rope of sufficient strength and long enough for the purpose. This I set about immediately, for, having the sacking of a bed that wanted mending, I sent it out of the palace by a lad whom I could trust, with orders to bring it back repaired, and to wrap up the proper length of rope inside.

When all was prepared, one evening, at supper-time, I went to the Queen my mother, who supped alone in her own apartment, it being fast-day and the King eating no supper. My brother, who on most occasions was patient and discreet, spurred on by the indignities he had received, and anxious to extricate himself from danger and regain his liberty, came to me as I was rising from table, and whispered to me to make haste and come to him in my own apartment. M. de Matignon, at that time a marshal, a sly, cunning Norman, and one who had no love for my brother, whether he had some knowledge of his design from some one who could not keep a secret, or only guessed at it, observed to the Queen my mother as she left the room (which I overheard, being near her, and circumspectly watching every word and motion, as may well be imagined, situated as I was betwixt fear and hope, and involved in perplexity) that my brother had undoubtedly an intention of withdrawing himself, and would not be there the next day; adding that he was assured of it, and she might take her measures accordingly.

I observed that she was much disconcerted by this observation, and I had my fears lest we should be discovered. When we came into her closet, she drew me aside and asked if I heard what Matignon had said.

I replied: "I did not hear it, Madame, but I observe that it has given you uneasiness."

"Yes," said she, "a great deal of uneasiness, for you know I have pledged myself to the King that your brother shall not depart hence, and Matignon has declared that he knows very well he will not be here to-morrow."

I now found myself under a great embarrassment; I was in danger either of
proving unfaithful to my brother, and thereby bringing his life into jeopardy, or of being obliged to declare that to be truth which I knew to
be false, and this I would have died rather than be guilty of.

In this extremity, if I had not been aided by God, my countenance, without speaking, would plainly have discovered what I wished to conceal. But God, who assists those who mean well, and whose divine goodness was discoverable in my brother's escape, enabled me to compose my looks and suggested to me such a reply as gave her to understand no more than I wished her to know, and cleared my conscience from making any declaration contrary to the truth. I answered her in these words:

"You cannot, Madame, but be sensible that M. de Matignon is not one of my brother's friends, and that he is, besides, a busy, meddling kind of man, who is sorry to find a reconciliation has taken place with us; and, as to my brother, I will answer for him with my life in case he goes hence, of which, if he had any design, I should, as I am well assured, not be ignorant, he never having yet concealed anything he meant to do from me."

All this was said by me with the assurance that, after my brother's escape, they would not dare to do me any injury; and in case of the worst, and when we should be discovered, I had much rather pledge my life than hazard my soul by a false declaration, and endanger my brother's life. Without scrutinising the import of my speech, she replied: "Remember what you now say,—you will be bound for him on the penalty of your life."

I smiled and answered that such was my intention. Then, wishing her a good night, I retired to my own bedchamber, where, undressing myself in haste and getting into bed, in order to dismiss the ladies and maids of honour, and there then remaining only my chamber-women, my brother came in, accompanied by Simier and Cange. Rising from my bed, we made the cord fast, and having looked out, at the window to discover if any one was in the ditch, with the assistance of three of my women, who slept in my room, and the lad who had brought in the rope, we let down my brother, who laughed and joked upon the occasion without the least apprehension, notwithstanding the height was considerable. We next lowered Simier into the ditch, who was in such a fright that he had scarcely strength to hold the rope fast; and lastly descended my brother's valet de chambre, Cange.

Through God's providence my brother got off undiscovered, and going to Ste. Genevieve, he found Bussi waiting there for him. By consent of the abbot, a hole had been made in the city wall, through which they passed, and horses being provided and in waiting, they mounted, and reached Angers without the least accident.

Whilst we were lowering down Cange, who, as I mentioned before, was the last, we observed a man rising out of the ditch, who ran towards the lodge adjoining to the tennis-court, in the direct way leading to the guard-house. I had no apprehensions on my own account, all my fears being absorbed by those I entertained for my brother; and now I was almost dead with alarm, supposing this might be a spy placed there by M. de Matignon, and that my brother would be taken. Whilst I was in this cruel state of anxiety, which can be judged of only by those who have experienced a similar situation, my women took a precaution for my safety and their own, which did not suggest itself to me. This was to burn the rope, that it might not appear to our conviction in case the man in question had been placed there to watch us. This rope occasioned so great a flame in burning, that it set fire to the chimney, which, being seen from without, alarmed the guard, who ran to us, knocking violently at the door, calling for it to be opened.

I now concluded that my brother was stopped, and that we were both undone. However, as, by the blessing of God and through his divine mercy alone, I have, amidst every danger with which I have been repeatedly surrounded, constantly preserved a presence of mind which directed what was best to be done, and observing that the rope was not more than half consumed, I told my women to go to the door, and speaking softly, as if I was asleep, to ask the men what they wanted. They did so, and the archers replied that the chimney was on fire, and they came to extinguish it. My women answered it was of no consequence, and they could put it out themselves, begging them not to awake me. This alarm thus passed off quietly, and they went away; but, in two hours afterward, M. de Cosse came for me to go to the King and the Queen, my mother, to give an account of my brother's escape, of which they had received intelligence by the Abbot of Ste. Genevieve.

It seems it had been concerted betwixt my brother and the abbot, in order to prevent the latter from falling under disgrace, that, when my brother might be supposed to have reached a sufficient distance, the abbot should go to Court, and say that he had been put into confinement whilst the hole was being made, and that he came to inform the King as soon as he had released himself.

I was in bed, for it was yet night; and rising hastily, I put on my night-clothes. One of my women was indiscreet enough to hold me round the waist, and exclaim aloud, shedding a flood of tears, that she should never see me more. M. de Cosse, pushing her away, said to me: "If I were not a person thoroughly devoted to your service, this woman has said enough to bring you into trouble. But," continued he, "fear nothing. God be praised, by this time the Prince your brother is out of danger."

These words were very necessary, in the present state of my mind, to fortify it against the reproaches and threats I had reason to expect from the King. I found him sitting at the foot of the Queen my mother's bed, in such a violent rage that I am inclined to believe I should have felt the effects of it, had he not been restrained by the absence of my brother and my mother's presence. They both told me that I had assured them my brother would not leave the Court, and that I pledged myself for his stay. I replied that it was true that he had deceived me, as he had them; however, I was ready still to pledge my life that his departure would not operate to the prejudice of the King's service, and that it would appear he was only gone to his own principality to give orders and forward his expedition to Flanders.

The King appeared to be somewhat mollified by this declaration, and now gave me permission to return to my own apartments. Soon afterwards he received letters from my brother, containing assurances of his attachment, in the terms I had before expressed. This caused a cessation of complaints, but by no means removed the King's dissatisfaction, who made a show of affording assistance to his expedition, but was secretly using every means to frustrate and defeat it.

LETTER XX.

Queen Marguerite Permitted to Go to the King Her Husband. — Is Accompanied
by the Queenmother. — Marguerite Insulted by Her Husband's Secretary. — She
Harbours Jealousy. — Her Attention to the King Her Husband during an
Indisposition. — Their Reconciliation. — The War Breaks Out
Afresh. — Affront Received from Marechal de Biron.

I now renewed my application for leave to go to the King my husband, which I continued to press on every opportunity. The King, perceiving that he could not refuse my leave any longer, was willing I should depart satisfied. He had this further view in complying with my wishes, that by this means he should withdraw me from my attachment to my brother. He therefore strove to oblige me in every way he could think of, and, to fulfil the promise made by the Queen my mother at the Peace of Sens, he gave me an assignment of my portion in territory, with the power of nomination to all vacant benefices and all offices; and, over and above the customary pension to the daughters of France, he gave another out of his privy purse.

He daily paid me a visit in my apartment, in which he took occasion to represent to me how useful his friendship would be to me; whereas that of my brother could be only injurious, — with arguments of the like kind.

However, all he could say was insufficient to prevail on me to swerve from the fidelity I had vowed to observe to my brother. The King was able to draw from me no other declaration than this: that it ever was, and should be, my earnest wish to see my brother firmly established in his gracious favour, which he had never appeared to me to have forfeited; that I was well assured he would exert himself to the utmost to regain it by every act of duty and meritorious service; that, with respect to myself, I thought I was so much obliged to him for the great honour he did me by repeated acts of generosity, that he might be assured, when I was with the King my husband I should consider myself bound in duty to obey all such commands as he should be pleased to give me; and that it would be my whole study to maintain the King my husband in a submission to his pleasure.

My brother was now on the point of leaving Alencon to go to Flanders; the Queen my mother was desirous to see him before his departure. I begged the King to permit me to take the opportunity of accompanying her to take leave of my brother, which he granted; but, as it seemed, with great unwillingness. When we returned from Alencon, I solicited the King to permit me to take leave of himself, as I had everything prepared for my journey. The Queen my mother being desirous to go to Gascony, where her presence was necessary for the King's service, was unwilling that I should depart without her. When we left Paris, the King accompanied us on the way as far as his palace of Dolinville. There we stayed with him a few days, and there we took our leave, and in a little time reached Guienne, which belonging to, and being under the government of the King my husband, I was everywhere received as Queen. My husband gave the Queen my mother a meeting at Wolle, which was held by the Huguenots as a cautionary town; and the country not being sufficiently quieted, she was permitted to go no further.

It was the intention of the Queen my mother to make but a short stay; but so many accidents arose from disputes betwixt the Huguenots and Catholics, that she was under the necessity of stopping there eighteen months. As this was very much against her inclination, she was sometimes inclined to think there was a design to keep her, in order to have the company of her maids of honour. For my husband had been greatly smitten with Dayelle, and M. de Thurene was in love with La Vergne. However, I received every mark of honour and attention from the King that I could expect or desire. He related to me, as soon as we met, the artifices which had been put in practice whilst he remained at Court to create a misunderstanding betwixt him and me; all this, he said, he knew was with a design to cause a rupture betwixt my brother and him, and thereby ruin us all three, as there was an exceeding great jealousy entertained of the friendship which existed betwixt us.

We remained in the disagreeable situation I have before described all the time the Queen my mother stayed in Gascony; but, as soon as she could reestablish peace, she, by desire of the King my husband, removed the King's lieutenant, the Marquis de Villars, putting in his place the Marechal de Biron. She then departed for Languedoc, and we conducted her to Castelnaudary; where, taking our leave, we returned to Pau, in Bearn; in which place, the Catholic religion not being tolerated, I was only allowed to have mass celebrated in a chapel of about three or four feet in length, and so narrow that it could scarcely hold seven or eight persons. During the celebration of mass, the bridge of the castle was drawn up to prevent the Catholics of the town and country from coming to assist at it; who having been, for some years, deprived of the benefit of following their own mode of worship, would have gladly been present. Actuated by so holy and laudable a desire, some of the inhabitants of Pau, on Whitsunday, found means to get into the castle before the bridge was drawn up, and were present at the celebration of mass, not being discovered until it was nearly over. At length the Huguenots espied them, and ran to acquaint Le Pin, secretary to the King my husband, who was greatly in his favour, and who conducted the whole business relating to the new religion. Upon receiving this intelligence, Le Pin ordered the guard to arrest these poor people, who were severely beaten in my presence, and afterwards locked up in prison, whence they were not released without paying a considerable fine.

This indignity gave me great offence, as I never expected anything of the kind. Accordingly, I complained of it to the King my husband, begging him to give orders for the release of these poor Catholics, who did not deserve to be punished for coming to my chapel to hear mass, a celebration of which they had been so long deprived of the benefit. Le Pin, with the greatest disrespect to his master, took upon him to reply, without waiting to hear what the King had to say. He told me that I ought not to trouble the King my husband about such matters; that what had been done was very right and proper; that those people had justly merited the treatment they met with, and all I could say would go for nothing, for it must be so; and that I ought to rest satisfied with being permitted to have mass said to me and my servants. This insolent speech from a person of his inferior condition incensed me greatly, and I entreated the King my husband, if I had the least share in his good graces, to do me justice, and avenge the insult offered me by this low man.

The King my husband, perceiving that I was offended, as I had reason to be, with this gross indignity, ordered Le Pin to quit our presence immediately; and, expressing his concern at his secretary's behaviour, who, he said, was overzealous in the cause of religion, he promised that he would make an example of him. As to the Catholic prisoners, he said he would advise with his parliament what ought to be done for my satisfaction.

Having said this, he went to his closet, where he found Le Pin, who, by dint of persuasion, made him change his resolution; insomuch that, fearing I should insist upon his dismissing his secretary, he avoided meeting me. At last, finding that I was firmly resolved to leave him, unless he dismissed Le Pin, he took advice of some persons, who, having themselves a dislike to the secretary, represented that he ought not to give me cause of displeasure for the sake of a man of his small importance,—especially one who, like him, had given me just reason to be offended; that, when it became known to the King my brother and the Queen my mother, they would certainly take it ill that he had not only not resented it, but, on the contrary, still kept him near his person.

This counsel prevailed with him, and he at length discarded his secretary. The King, however, continued to behave to me with great coolness, being influenced, as he afterwards confessed, by the counsel of M. de Pibrac, who acted the part of a double dealer, telling me that I ought not to pardon an affront offered by such a mean fellow, but insist upon his being dismissed; whilst he persuaded the King my husband that there was no reason for parting with a man so useful to him, for such a trivial cause. This was done by M. de Pibrac, thinking I might be induced, from such mortifications, to return to France, where he enjoyed the offices of president and King's counsellor.

I now met with a fresh cause for disquietude in my present situation, for, Dayelle being gone, the King my husband placed his affections on Rebours. She was an artful young person, and had no regard for me; accordingly, she did me all the ill offices in her power with him. In the midst of these trials, I put my trust in God, and he, moved with pity by my tears, gave permission for our leaving Pau, that "little Geneva;" and, fortunately for me, Rebours was taken ill and stayed behind. The King my husband no sooner lost sight of her than he forgot her; he now turned his eyes and attention towards Fosseuse. She was much handsomer than the other, and was at that time young, and really a very amiable person.

Pursuing the road to Montauban, we stopped at a little town called Eause, where, in the night, the King my husband was attacked with a high fever, accompanied with most violent pains in his head. This fever lasted for seventeen days, during which time he had no rest night or day, but was continually removed from one bed to another. I nursed him the whole time, never stirring from his bedside, and never putting off my clothes. He took notice of my extraordinary tenderness, and spoke of it to several persons, and particularly to my cousin M— —-, who, acting the part of an affectionate relation, restored me to his favour, insomuch that I never stood so highly in it before. This happiness I had the good fortune to enjoy during the four or five years that I remained with him in Gascony.

Our residence, for the most part of the time I have mentioned, was at Nerac, where our Court was so brilliant that we had no cause to regret our absence from the Court of France. We had with us the Princesse de Navarre, my husband's sister, since married to the Duc de Bar; there were besides a number of ladies belonging to myself. The King my husband was attended by a numerous body of lords and gentlemen, all as gallant persons as I have seen in any Court; and we had only to lament that they were Huguenots. This difference of religion, however, caused no dispute among us; the King my husband and the Princess his sister heard a sermon, whilst I and my servants heard mass. I had a chapel in the park for the purpose, and, as soon as the service of both religions was over, we joined company in a beautiful garden, ornamented with long walks shaded with laurel and cypress trees. Sometimes we took a walk in the park on the banks of the river, bordered by an avenue of trees three thousand yards in length. The rest of the day was passed in innocent amusements; and in the afternoon, or at night, we commonly had a ball.

The King was very assiduous with Fosseuse, who, being dependent on me, kept herself within the strict bounds of honour and virtue. Had she always done so, she had not brought upon herself a misfortune which has proved of such fatal consequence to myself as well as to her.

But our happiness was too great to be of long continuance, and fresh troubles broke out betwixt the King my husband and the Catholics, and gave rise to a new war. The King my husband and the Marechal de Biron, who was the King's lieutenant in Guienne, had a difference, which was aggravated by the Huguenots. This breach became in a short time so wide that all my efforts to close it were useless. They made their separate complaints to the King. The King my husband insisted on the removal of the Marechal de Biron, and the Marshal charged the King my husband, and the rest of those who were of the pretended reformed religion, with designs contrary to peace. I saw, with great concern, that affairs were likely soon to come to an open rupture; and I had no power to prevent it.

The Marshal advised the King to come to Guienne himself, saying that in his presence matters might be settled. The Huguenots, hearing of this proposal, supposed the King would take possession of their towns, and, thereupon, came to a resolution to take up arms. This was what I feared; I was become a sharer in the King my husband's fortune, and was now to be in opposition to the King my brother and the religion I had been bred up in. I gave my opinion upon this war to the King my husband and his Council, and strove to dissuade them from engaging in it. I represented to them the hazards of carrying on a war when they were to be opposed against so able a general as the Marechal de Biron, who would not spare them, as other generals had done, he being their private enemy. I begged them to consider that, if the King brought his whole force against them, with intention to exterminate their religion, it would not be in their power to oppose or prevent it. But they were so headstrong, and so blinded with the hope of succeeding in the surprise of certain towns in Languedoc and Gascony, that, though the King did me the honour, upon all occasions, to listen to my advice, as did most of the Huguenots, yet I could not prevail on them to follow it in the present situation of affairs, until it was too late, and after they had found, to their cost, that my counsel was good. The torrent was now burst forth, and there was no possibility of stopping its course until it had spent its utmost strength.

Before that period arrived, foreseeing the consequences, I had often written to the King and the Queen my mother, to offer something to the King my husband by way of accommodating matters. But they were bent against it, and seemed to be pleased that matters had taken such a turn, being assured by Marechal de Biron that he had it in his power to crush the Huguenots whenever he pleased. In this crisis my advice was not attended to, the dissensions increased, and recourse was had to arms.

The Huguenots had reckoned upon a force more considerable than they were able to collect together, and the King my husband found himself outnumbered by Marechal de Biron. In consequence, those of the pretended reformed religion failed in all their plans, except their attack upon Cahors, which they took with petards, after having lost a great number of men, M. de Vezins, who commanded in the town, disputing their entrance for two or three days, from street to street, and even from house to house. The King my husband displayed great valour and conduct upon the occasion, and showed himself to be a gallant and brave general. Though the Huguenots succeeded in this attempt, their loss was so great that they gained nothing from it. Marechal de Biron kept the field, and took every place that declared for the Huguenots, putting all that opposed him to the sword.

From the commencement of this war, the King my husband doing me the honour to love me, and commanding me not to leave him, I had resolved to share his fortune, not without extreme regret, in observing that this war was of such a nature that I could not, in conscience, wish success to either side; for if the Huguenots got the upper hand, the religion which I cherished as much as my life was lost, and if the Catholics prevailed, the King my husband was undone. But, being thus attached to my husband, by the duty I owed him, and obliged by the attentions he was pleased to show me, I could only acquaint the King and the Queen my mother with the situation to which I was reduced, occasioned by my advice to them not having been attended to. I, therefore, prayed them, if they could not extinguish the flames of war in the midst of which I was placed, at least to give orders to Marechal de Biron to consider the town I resided in, and three leagues round it, as neutral ground, and that I would get the King my husband to do the same. This the King granted me for Nerac, provided my husband was not there; but if he should enter it, the neutrality was to cease, and so to remain as long as he continued there. This convention was observed, on both sides, with all the exactness I could desire. However, the King my husband was not to be prevented from often visiting Nerac, which was the residence of his sister and me. He was fond of the society of ladies, and, moreover, was at that time greatly enamoured with Fosseuse, who held the place in his affections which Rebours had lately occupied. Fosseuse did me no ill offices, so that the King my husband and I continued to live on very good terms, especially as he perceived me unwilling to oppose his inclinations.

Led by such inducements, he came to Nerac, once, with a body of troops, and stayed three days, not being able to leave the agreeable company he found there. Marechal de Biron, who wished for nothing so much as such an opportunity, was apprised of it, and, under pretence of joining M. de Cornusson, the seneschal of Toulouse, who was expected with a reinforcement for his army, he began his march; but, instead of pursuing the road, according to the orders he had issued, he suddenly ordered his troops to file off towards Nerac, and, before nine in the morning, his whole force was drawn up within sight of the town, and within cannon-shot of it.

The King my husband had received intelligence, the evening before, of the expected arrival of M. de Cornusson, and was desirous of preventing the junction, for which purpose he resolved to attack him and the Marshal separately. As he had been lately joined by M. de La Rochefoucauld, with a corps of cavalry consisting of eight hundred men, formed from the nobility of Saintonge, he found himself sufficiently strong to undertake such a plan. He, therefore, set out before break of day to make his attack as they crossed the river. But his intelligence did not prove to be correct, for De Cornusson passed it the evening before. My husband, being thus disappointed in his design, returned to Nerac, and entered at one gate just as Marechal de Biron drew up his troops before the other. There fell so heavy a rain at that moment that the musketry was of no use. The King my husband, however, threw a body of his troops into a vineyard to stop the Marshal's progress, not being able to do more on account of the unfavourableness of the weather.

In the meantime, the Marshal continued with his troops drawn up in order of battle, permitting only two or three of his men to advance, who challenged a like number to break lances in honour of their mistresses. The rest of the army kept their ground, to mask their artillery, which, being ready to play, they opened to the right and left, and fired seven or eight shots upon the town, one of which struck the palace. The Marshal, having done this, marched off, despatching a trumpeter to me with his excuse. He acquainted me that, had I been alone, he would on no account have fired on the town; but the terms of neutrality for the town, agreed upon by the King, were, as I well knew, in case the King my husband should not be found in it, and, if otherwise, they were void. Besides which, his orders were to attack the King my husband wherever he should find him.

I must acknowledge on every other occasion the Marshal showed me the greatest respect, and appeared to be much my friend. During the war my letters have frequently fallen into his hands, when he as constantly forwarded them to me unopened. And whenever my people have happened to be taken prisoners by his army, they were always well treated as soon as they mentioned to whom they belonged.

I answered his message by the trumpeter, saying that I well knew what he had done was strictly agreeable to the convention made and the orders he had received, but that a gallant officer like him would know how to do his duty without giving his friends cause of offence; that he might have permitted me the enjoyment of the King my husband's company in Nerac for three days, adding, that he could not attack him, in my presence, without attacking me; and concluding that, certainly, I was greatly offended by his conduct, and would take the first opportunity of making my complaint to the King my brother.

LETTER XXI.

Situation of Affairs in Flanders. — Peace Brought About by Duc d'Alencon's
Negotiation. — Marechal de Biron Apologises for Firing on Nerac. — Henri
Desperately in Love with Fosseuse. — Queen Marguerite Discovers Fosseuse
to Be Pregnant, Which She Denies. — Fosseuse in Labour. Marguerite's
Generous Behaviour to Her. — Marguerite's Return to Paris.

The war lasted some time longer, but with disadvantage to the Huguenots. The King my husband at length became desirous to make a peace. I wrote on the subject to the King and the Queen my mother; but so elated were they both with Marechal de Biron's success that they would not agree to any terms.

About the time this war broke out, Cambray, which had been delivered up to my brother by M. d'Ainsi, according to his engagement with me, as I have before related, was besieged by the forces of Spain. My brother received the news of this siege at his castle of Plessis-les-Tours, whither he had retired after his return from Flanders, where, by the assistance of the Comte de Lalain, he had been invested with the government of Mons, Valenciennes, and their dependencies.

My brother, being anxious to relieve Cambray, set about raising an army, with all the expedition possible; but, finding it could not be accomplished very speedily, he sent forward a reinforcement under the command of M. de Balagny, to succour the place until he arrived himself with a sufficient force to raise the siege. Whilst he was in the midst of these preparations this Huguenot war broke out, and the men he had raised left him to incorporate themselves with the King's army, which had reached Gascony.

My brother was now without hope of raising the siege, and to lose Cambray would be attended with the loss of the other countries he had just obtained. Besides, what he should regret more, such losses would reduce to great straits M. de Balagny and the gallant troops so nobly defending the place.

His grief on this occasion was poignant, and, as his excellent judgment furnished him with expedients under all his difficulties, he resolved to endeavour to bring about a peace. Accordingly he despatched a gentleman to the King with his advice to accede to terms, offering to undertake the treaty himself. His design in offering himself as negotiator was to prevent the treaty being drawn out to too great a length, as might be the case if confided to others. It was necessary that he should speedily relieve Cambray, for M. de Balagny, who had thrown himself into the city as I have before mentioned, had written to him that he should be able to defend the place for six months; but, if he received no succours within that time, his provisions would be all expended, and he should be obliged to give way to the clamours of the inhabitants, and surrender the town.

By God's favour, the King was induced to listen to my brother's proposal of undertaking a negotiation for a peace. The King hoped thereby to disappoint him in his expectations in Flanders, which he never had approved. Accordingly he sent word back to my brother that he should accept his proffer of negotiating a peace, and would send him for his coadjutors, M. de Villeroy and M. de Bellievre. The commission my brother was charged with succeeded, and, after a stay of seven months in Gascony, he settled a peace and left us, his thoughts being employed during the whole time on the means of relieving Cambray, which the satisfaction he found in being with us could not altogether abate.

The peace my brother, made, as I have just mentioned, was so judiciously framed that it gave equal satisfaction to the King and the Catholics, and to the King my husband and the Huguenots, and obtained him the affections of both parties. He likewise acquired from it the assistance of that able general, Marechal de Biron, who undertook the command of the army destined to raise the siege of Cambray. The King my husband was equally gratified in the Marshal's removal from Gascony and having Marechal de Matignon in his place.

Before my brother set off he was desirous to bring about a reconciliation betwixt the King my husband and Mareohal de Biron, provided the latter should make his apologies to me for his conduct at Nerac. My brother had desired me to treat him with all disdain, but I used this hasty advice with discretion, considering that my brother might one day or other repent having given it, as he had everything to hope, in his present situation, from the bravery of this officer.

My brother returned to France accompanied by Marechal de Biron. By his negotiation of a peace he had acquired to himself great credit with both parties, and secured a powerful force for the purpose of raising the siege of Cambray. But honours and success are followed by envy. The King beheld this accession of glory to his brother with great dissatisfaction. He had been for seven months, while my brother and I were together in Gascony, brooding over his malice, and produced the strangest invention that can be imagined. He pretended to believe (what the King my husband can easily prove to be false) that I instigated him to go to war that I might procure for my brother the credit of making peace. This is not at all probable when it is considered the prejudice my brother's affairs in, Flanders sustained by the war.

But envy and malice are self-deceivers, and pretend to discover what no one else can perceive. On this frail foundation the King raised an altar of hatred, on which he swore never to cease till he had accomplished my brother's ruin and mine. He had never forgiven me for the attachment I had discovered for my brother's interest during the time he was in Poland and since.

Fortune chose to favour the King's animosity; for, during the seven months that my brother stayed in Gascony, he conceived a passion for Fosseuse, who was become the doting piece of the King my husband, as I have already mentioned, since he had quitted Rebours. This new passion in my brother had induced the King my husband to treat me with coldness, supposing that I countenanced my brother's addresses. I no sooner discovered this than I remonstrated with my brother, as I knew he would make every sacrifice for my repose. I begged him to give over his pursuit, and not to speak to her again. I succeeded this way to defeat the malice of my ill-fortune; but there was still behind another secret ambush, and that of a more fatal nature; for Fosseuse, who was passionately fond of the King my husband, but had hitherto granted no favours inconsistent with prudence and modesty, piqued by his jealousy of my brother, gave herself up suddenly to his will, and unfortunately became pregnant. She no sooner made this discovery, than she altered her conduct towards me entirely from what it was before. She now shunned my presence as much as she had been accustomed to seek it, and whereas before she strove to do me every good office with the King my husband, she now endeavoured to make all the mischief she was able betwixt us. For his part, he avoided me; he grew cold and indifferent, and since Fosseuse ceased to conduct herself with discretion, the happy moments that we experienced during the four or five years we were together in Gascony were no more.

Peace being restored, and my brother departed for France, as I have already related, the King my husband and I returned to Nerac. We were no sooner there than Fosseuse persuaded the King my husband to make a journey to the waters of Aigues-Caudes, in Bearn, perhaps with a design to rid herself of her burden there. I begged the King my husband to excuse my accompanying him, as, since the affront that I had received at Pau, I had made a vow never to set foot in Bearn until the Catholic religion was reestablished there. He pressed me much to go with him, and grew angry at my persisting to refuse his request. He told me that his little girl (for so he affected to call Fosseuse) was desirous to go there on account of a colic, which she felt frequent returns of. I answered that I had no objection to his taking her with him. He then said that she could not go unless I went; that it would occasion scandal, which might as well be avoided. He continued to press me to accompany him, but at length I prevailed with him to consent to go without me, and to take her with him, and, with her, two of her companions, Rebours and Ville-Savin, together with the governess. They set out accordingly, and I waited their return at Baviere.

I had every day news from Rebours, informing me how matters went. This Rebours I have mentioned before to have been the object of my husband's passion, but she was now cast off, and, consequently, was no friend to Fosseuse, who had gained that place in his affection she had before held. She, therefore, strove all she could to circumvent her; and, indeed, she was fully qualified for such a purpose, as she was a cunning, deceitful young person. She gave me to understand that Fosseuse laboured to do me every ill office in her power; that she spoke of me with the greatest disrespect on all occasions, and expressed her expectations of marrying the King herself, in case she should be delivered of a son, when I was to be divorced. She had said, further, that when the King my husband returned to Baviere, he had resolved to go to Pau, and that I should go with him, whether I would or not.

This intelligence was far from being agreeable to me, and I knew not what to think of it. I trusted in the goodness of God, and I had a reliance on the generosity of the King my husband; yet I passed the time I waited for his return but uncomfortably, and often thought I shed more tears than they drank water. The Catholic nobility of the neighbourhood of Baviere used their utmost endeavours to divert my chagrin, for the month or five weeks that the King my husband and Fosseuse stayed at Aigues-Caudes.

On his return, a certain nobleman acquainted the King my husband with the concern I was under lest he should go to Pau, whereupon he did not press me on the subject, but only said he should have been glad if I had consented to go with him. Perceiving, by my tears and the expressions I made use of, that I should prefer even death to such a journey, he altered his intentions and we returned to Nerac.

The pregnancy of Fosseuse was now no longer a secret. The whole Court talked of it, and not only the Court, but all the country. I was willing to prevent the scandal from spreading, and accordingly resolved to talk to her on the subject. With this resolution, I took her into my closet, and spoke to her thus: "Though you have for some time estranged yourself from me, and, as it has been reported to me, striven to do me many ill offices with the King my husband, yet the regard I once had for you, and the esteem which I still entertain for those honourable persons to whose family you belong, do not admit of my neglecting to afford you all the assistance in my power in pour present unhappy situation. I beg you, therefore, not to conceal the truth, it being both for your interest and mine, under whose protection you are, to declare it. Tell me the truth, and I will act towards you as a mother. You know that a contagious disorder has broken out in the place, and, under pretence of avoiding it, I will go to Mas-d'Agenois, which is a house belonging to the King my husband, in a very retired situation. I will take you with me, and such other persons as you shall name. Whilst we are there, the King will take the diversion of hunting in some other part of the country, and I shall not stir thence before your delivery. By this means we shall put a stop to the scandalous reports which are now current, and which concern you more than myself."

So far from showing any contrition, or returning thanks for my kindness, she replied, with the utmost arrogance, that she would prove all those to be liars who had reported such things of her; that, for my part, I had ceased for a long time to show her any marks of regard, and she saw that I was determined upon her ruin. These words she delivered in as loud a tone as mine had been mildly expressed; and, leaving me abruptly, she flew in a rage to the King my husband, to relate to him what I had said to her. He was very angry upon the occasion, and declared he would make them all liars who had laid such things to her charge. From that moment until the hour of her delivery, which was a few months after, he never spoke to me.

She found the pains of labour come upon her about daybreak, whilst she was in bed in the chamber where the maids of honour slept. She sent for my physician, and begged him to go and acquaint the King my husband that she was taken ill. We slept in separate beds in the same chamber, and had done so for some time.

The physician delivered the message as he was directed, which greatly embarrassed my husband. What to do he did not know. On the one hand, he was fearful of a discovery; on the other, he foresaw that, without proper assistance, there was danger of losing one he so much loved. In this dilemma, he resolved to apply to me, confess all, and implore my aid and advice, well knowing that, notwithstanding what had passed, I should be ready to do him a pleasure. Having come to this resolution, he withdrew my curtains, and spoke to me thus: "My dear, I have concealed a matter from you which I now confess. I beg you to forgive me, and to think no more about what I have said to you on the subject. Will you oblige me so far as to rise and go to Fosseuse, who is taken very ill? I am well assured that, in her present situation, you will forget everything and resent nothing. You know how dearly I love her, and I hope you will comply with my request." I answered that I had too great a respect for him to be offended at anything he should do, and that I would go to her immediately, and do as much for her as if she were a child of my own. I advised him, in the meantime, to go out and hunt, by which means he would draw away all his people, and prevent tattling.

I removed Fosseuse, with all convenient haste, from the chamber in which the maids of honour were, to one in a more retired part of the palace, got a physician and some women about her, and saw that she wanted for nothing that was proper in her situation. It pleased God that she should bring forth a daughter, since dead. As soon as she was delivered I ordered her to be taken back to the chamber from which she had been brought. Notwithstanding these precautions, it was not possible to prevent the story from circulating through the palace. When the King my husband returned from hunting he paid her a visit, according to custom. She begged that I might come and see her, as was usual with me when any one of my maids of honour was taken ill. By this means she expected to put a stop to stories to her prejudice. The King my husband came from her into my bedchamber, and found me in bed, as I was fatigued and required rest, after having been called up so early.

He begged me to get up and pay her a visit. I told him I went according to his desire before, when she stood in need of assistance, but now she wanted no help; that to visit her at this time would be only exposing her more, and cause myself to be pointed at by all the world. He seemed to be greatly displeased at what I said, which vexed me the more as I thought I did not deserve such treatment after what I had done at his request in the morning; she likewise contributed all in her power to aggravate matters betwixt him and me.

In the meantime, the King my brother, always well informed of what is passing in the families of the nobility of his kingdom, was not ignorant of the transactions of our Court. He was particularly curious to learn everything that happened with us, and knew every minute circumstance that I have now related. Thinking this a favourable occasion to wreak his vengeance on me for having been the means of my brother acquiring so much reputation by the peace he had brought about, he made use of the accident that happened in our Court to withdraw me from the King my husband, and thereby reduce me to the state of misery he wished to plunge me in. To this purpose he prevailed on the Queen my mother to write to me, and express her anxious desire to see me after an absence of five or six years. She added that a journey of this sort to Court would be serviceable to the affairs of the King my husband as well as my own; that the King my brother himself was desirous of seeing me, and that if I wanted money for the journey he would send it me. The King wrote to the same purpose, and despatched Manique, the steward of his household, with instructions to use every persuasion with me to undertake the journey. The length of time I had been absent in Gascony, and the unkind usage I received on account of Fosseuse, contributed to induce me to listen to the proposal made me.

The King and the Queen both wrote to me. I received three letters, in quick succession; and, that I might have no pretence for staying, I had the sum of fifteen hundred crowns paid me to defray the expenses of my journey. The Queen my mother wrote that she would give me the meeting in Saintonge, and that, if the King my husband would accompany me so far, she would treat with him there, and give him every satisfaction with respect to the King. But the King and she were desirous to have him at their Court, as he had been before with my brother; and the Marechal de Matignon had pressed the matter with the King, that he might have no one to interfere with him in Gascony. I had had too long experience of what was to be expected at their Court to hope much from all the fine promises that were made to me. I had resolved, however, to avail myself of the opportunity of an absence of a few months, thinking it might prove the means of setting matters to rights. Besides which, I thought that, as I should take Fosseuse with me, it was possible that the King's passion for her might cool when she was no longer in his sight, or he might attach himself to some other that was less inclined to do me mischief.

It was with some difficulty that the King my husband would consent to a removal, so unwilling was he to leave his Fosseuse. He paid more attention to me, in hopes that I should refuse to set out on this journey to France; but, as I had given my word in my letters to the King and the Queen my mother that I would go, and as I had even received money for the purpose, I could not do otherwise.

And herein my ill-fortune prevailed over the reluctance I had to leave the King my husband, after the instances of renewed love and regard which he had begun to show me.